• Bartholom

COUNTRY WALKS
AROUND LONDON

35 walks within 30 miles of London

Bartholomew

An Imprint of HarperCollins*Publishers*

CONTENTS

Location map/Key to route maps   3
Introduction   4

KENT

Walk 1   Riverside Country Park   12
Walk 2   Shorne Wood Country Park   13
Walk 3   Holly Hill   14
Walk 4   Hollingbourne Church to Leeds Castle   16
Walk 5   Knole Park   18
Walk 6   Groombridge and Harrison's Rocks   19
Walk 7   Penshurst   20
Walk 8   Chevening and District   22

SURREY

Walk 9   Farthing Downs   24
Walk 10   Juniper Bottom to Box Hill   25
Walk 11   Leith Hill   26
Walk 12   Shere and Hackhurst Downs   28
Walk 13   Winkworth Arboretum   30
Walk 14   Ockley Common   32
Walk 15   Brookwood   33

BERKSHIRE

Walk 16   Windsor Forest at Bracknell   34

Walk 17   Wraysbury Lakes   36
Walk 18   Henley-on-Thames   38

BUCKINGHAMSHIRE

Walk 19   Dorney and Boveney Lock   40
Walk 20   Denham   41
Walk 21   Cookham   42
Walk 22   Milton's Cottage   44
Walk 23   Hughenden Manor   46
Walk 24   Great Missenden   47

HERTFORDSHIRE

Walk 25   Tring Reservoirs   48
Walk 26   Telegraph Hill   49
Walk 27   Verulamium   50
Walk 28   Knebworth Park   52
Walk 29   Hertford   54
Walk 30   Widford   55

ESSEX

Walk 31   Epping Forest   56
Walk 32   Hatfield Forest   58
Walk 33   Ongar and Greensted   60
Walk 34   Thorndon Country Park   61
Walk 35   Benfleet and Leigh   62

A Bartholomew Walk Guide
Published by Bartholomew
An Imprint of HarperCollins*Publishers*
77-85 Fulham Palace Road
London W6 8JB

First published 1996
© Bartholomew 1996

Printed in Hong Kong

ISBN 0 7028 3141 7
96/1/16

LOCATION MAP

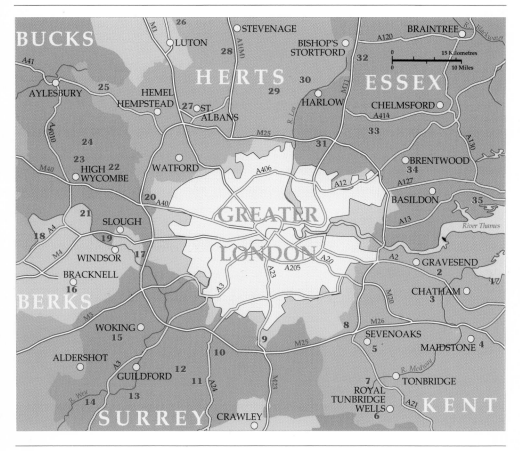

KEY TO ROUTE MAPS

═══════ Motorway	- - - - - Walk Route
═══════ Major Road	– – – – Alternative Route
═══════ Minor Road	· · · · · · · Other Footpath
= = = = = Track	∿ Stream/River
⊢⊢⊢⊙⊢⊢⊢ Railway/Station	▢ ▢ Built up-area/Building
❶ Route Description	Orchard
Ⓐ Point of Interest	Marsh
	Woodland

†	Church or Chapel
⟁	Picnic Site
☀	Viewpoint
WC	Public Toilet
PO	Post Office
PH	Public House
☎	Telephone
i	Tourist Information
P	Parking

INTRODUCTION

(Numbers in italics refer to routes described in this book.)

You want to get out of London and into the countryside at the weekend, but you don't know where to look for the best rural walking. Maybe you live in the Home Counties and want some guidance on where to go and what to look out for in your own area. The 35 walks described in this book are just a taster of what's available and accessible from each side of the metropolis. This introduction contains some pointers on where else to go walking around London. It gives a broad perspective on the types of terrain you will encounter, describes some of the highlights of each region and talks a little bit about some interesting points of history. Mention is also made of several long distance paths which can, of course, be walked in whole or part. Start with some of the walks in this book, then buy some maps and try devising your own routes!

Nature watching tips are included on pages 8-10. Guidelines for following these walks and other practical advice and information is given on pages 11-12.

South of the Thames

If one takes the mouth of the Thames as a starting point, a clockwise circuit around London both begins and ends with the rich wildlife habitat of the British estuary. In northern Kent, the broad outlet of the River Medway *(1)* is bordered by mud flats which attract seabirds, as do the estuaries near the Essex coast; further east in Kent, the marshes along the southern edge of the Isle of Sheppey and beside the muddy Swale estuary are renowned for their high concentration of birdlife.

Charles Dickens grew up in Chatham and the influence of his sometimes bleak and windswept native surroundings may be seen in several of his novels, such as *Great Expectations*. In *Pickwick Papers*, Dickens described one of his own favourite walks in Shorne Wood Country Park *(2)* near the picturesque village of Cobham. In spite of the proximity of a motorway and housing development, much of the area remains as it was in Dickens' time.

The geological make-up of the coastal strip is clay, sand and gravel, but not far inland this gives way to the chalk ridge of the North Downs *(3, 8, 10, 11, 12)*, which is virtually continuous from Farnham, in Surrey, to Dover. The narrow Hog's Back in the west broadens to a sweeping escarpment that dominates the landscape of south-east England and is ideal walking terrain. The gentle northern slopes are easy to climb and the views from the escarpment are highly rewarding.

Some of the well-worn paths have a long history due to the importance of the ridge as a communication route with the continent when travel across sparsely populated, forested southern England could be treacherous. The North Downs Way *(3, 8, 9, 12)*, which traces the crest of the downs for their entire length of 141 miles (227 km), originates from Neolithic times, as does the Pilgrim's Way *(3, 12)* which partly coincides with it (and is nearly as long, stretching from Winchester to Canterbury). This path also reflects the one-time importance of Winchester (England's Saxon capital) as well as Canterbury—a place of pilgrimage (famously documented by Chaucer in *Canterbury Tales*) after Thomas à Becket was murdered in Canterbury Cathedral in 1170.

The present geological pattern in the south-east, of a multi-layer sandwich, was created by upheavals and erosion so that layers of different rocks have revealed themselves in strips. The porous rocks of the North Downs and Greensand Hills (formed of green limestone and which also boast a long-distance path) made for dry walking (and still do) in contrast to the clay of the Weald. In addition, Stone Age peoples utilised the chalk for flint tools and in the Iron Age hill-top forts were built *(11)*.

In Kent, the Medway valley to the south of the downs is at the heart of the county's reputation as the 'garden of England' which traditionally supplied London with all its fruit and vegetables. The impermeable Wealden clays have given rise to a multitude of tributaries and drainage ditches across the flat fertile land. In addition to 'pick your own' orchards, hop gardens and vineyards are features of the countryside. Grown to give flavour to beer since late Medieval times, in the 19th century hops were dried in kilns known as oast-houses. These conical (or sometimes square) buildings have become a symbol of Kent's landscape, as was the annual influx of hand-pickers from the East End. Now most of the oasthouses have been converted into private homes.

Although Kent's coastal landmarks reflect the historical preoccupation of the peninsula with defence, inland in Kent and Surrey there is a wealth of grand and modest church and domestic architecture (2, 4–12) The latter county was sparsely populated until it became fashionable in the late 17th century to have a country retreat. A number of fine mansions were built (10, 11), spa towns grew up, hill-walking as a leisure pursuit was born on the North Downs, and public and private landscaped gardens and arboretums (13) became popular. The landscape aesthetics of 17th-century diarist, John Evelyn, impacted not only on his family estate in Wotton and other personal projects (11), but also on planting and landscaping schemes into the 19th century.

Surrey has retained extensive tracts of ancient woodland (the original meaning of 'weald' being 'forested land'), partly because the soils were deemed unsuitable for intensive agriculture. Nevertheless, the woods have long been managed for timber production, whereas infertile heathland (14) remains in its natural condition.

Local authorities now channel a lot of resources into countryside management. Walks in this area will benefit from a project launched by the Countryside Commission and Kent County Council to maintain and enhance the North Downs Way National Trail and significant landscape and historical features nearby. The High Weald Walk (6), a 27.5 mile (44 km) circuit of Tunbridge Wells, was opened in 1994. It was created by Kent and East Sussex County Councils mainly through the upgrading of existing rights of way.

The Thames Valley

The Thames itself is the focus of most walking opportunities to the immediate west of London, and the riverscape dominates the countryside as well as much of the urban development in this region. Of course, the river flows through a wide range of landscapes in the 215 miles (346 km) from its source near Kemble in rural Gloucestershire to the sea. Interested parties, including the Department of the Environment, are currently engaged in devising strategies to improve the appearance and status of the Thames banks in London, and the partial success of docklands regeneration is well documented. Concentrating, however, on the section of the river from Kingston-upon-Thames to the eastern border of Oxfordshire, it passes through woodland, meadows and charming villages (18, 19, 21), beyond which are rolling hills and more farmland. It is a landscape that inspired Turner and other painters of the English School.

In addition, there are a number of historically important towns (18, 21) which grew up beside the river in the days when commercial life was centred on the Thames. The major architectural landmarks along this stretch are significant too. They include: Hampton Court, regarded as 'England's Versaille'; Windsor Castle, a Norman fortification bordered on the south by the magnificent Windsor Great Park and Forest; and Eton Public School. On the Surrey side there is also Runnymede, the site where in 1215 King John was forced by the barons to sign the Magna Carta, a guarantee of privileges which became a byword for the subjects' liberty. Runnymede was at that time in Windsor Forest, which stretched from Surrey to Buckinghamshire and was the favourite hunting ground of William the Conqueror. This vast expanse of woodland has shrunk to 800 acres (323 hectares), mainly as a result of the Dissaforestation Act of 1817, which allowed much of the former woodland to be sold off or subsumed into the park.

The Chilterns rise above the Thames valley west of Henley-on-Thames, which is the at the edge of this book's geographical scope (18). Rainwater drains from the porous chalk hills (geologically similar to the North Downs) into the Thames.The Icknield Way (26) passes over the Chilterns then continues across the Berkshire Downs on the west of the Thames, where it is known as the Ridgeway. This prehistoric track once linked Wells-next-the-Sea in Norfolk to the Dorset coast!

The Romans were the first people to realise the Thames' potential as a commercial asset. They founded the city of Londinium (London), which grew into an international trading post and eventually, in the 19th century, became the largest port in the world. Until the mid 19th century, the most efficient way of transporting agricultural produce and other goods between London and neighbouring counties was by means of sailing barges along the Thames. In addition, weirs harnessed the river to power mills and facilitated a thriving fishing industry. (Eels, in particular, were plentiful; hence their popularity as part of the working-class Londoner's diet.) Canal building projects in the late 18th and 19th centuries succeeded in creating a countrywide network of waterways, but they quickly became obsolete for commercial purposes due to the advent of the railways. Instead, both the river and canals *(15, 25)* have become a playground for boating enthusiasts, and the legacy of the towpaths along their banks is many miles of pleasant walking.

The ground is, of course, level beside the Thames and the compacted clay soil is a firm, even surface to walk on when it is dry. Most of the length of the river has had a public footpath on one bank or the other for some years, but the Ramblers Association has campaigned for 20 years for the opening up of even more stretches of the riverside owned by local authorities and private landowners. The aim was to create a long distance walk along the length of the Thames, as far as possible without deviations away from the riverside. Since 1990 the Countryside Commission has been working towards this aim with the result that the Thames Path National Trail is scheduled to open in 1996. This trail will be 175 miles (282 km) long, ending at the Thames Flood Barrier.

It is hoped eventually to link the Thames Path with other towpaths. Meanwhile there is plenty of shorter distance walking to be done away from the primary river, concentrating on other wetlands in the Thames Valley *(17, 21)*. These are often of greater interest to the naturalist, are equally well served by footpaths, and can be more peaceful and picturesque than the bustling Thames. The River Colne, for example, splits from the Thames at Staines and runs northward, where its takes a parallel course to the Grand Union Canal for 10 miles (16 km). It has a myriad of tributaries, and beside the river is a series of flooded gravel pits. An instance of the relics of industry—in this case quarrying—being converted into environmentally desirable features, many have become Sites of Special Scientific Interest due to their wildfowl populations. Other artificial creations that have attracted wildlife include watercourses built to drain farmland (such as the Green Way featured in *Walk 21*) and the six large reservoirs in the southern Colne Valley that supply water to West London.

North of the Thames

Reference to the counties of Buckinghamshire, Hertfordshire and Essex may not inspire thoughts of beautiful unspoilt countryside, and parts of them have undeniably suffered from the encroachment of London's suburbs, industrialisation and population pressures caused by the influx of city commuters. Nevertheless, there is still a great deal of pleasant and varied countryside worth visiting in this region.

Buckinghamshire and Hertfordshire are small and populous, yet they possess: the beech wood covered Chiltern Hills and the tranquil Vale of Aylesbury on their far side; an attractive and interesting stretch of the walker-friendly Grand Union Canal *(25)*; prosperous estates with enviable expanses of parkland and imposing manors *(23, 28)*; and wooded heathland in the east. The demands of the 'stockbroker belt' population have resulted in the establishment of excellent public transport links, which is good news for walkers *(Walks 20, 24, 27* and *29* can all be reached by a direct train from London), and the efforts of the Chiltern Society have ensured that paths in the hills are well maintained.

One of the most important canals in Britain passes through the western end of this region. The Grand Union Canal *(25)* stretches for 138 miles (222 km) from Little Venice, in London, to Birmingham. Begun at the peak of canal mania in 1793, the Grand Union is a remarkable feat of construction. In its time, it was a vital industrial transport link whose role was comparable to that of the M1 now. Since 1993 there has been a National Trail running alongside the canal for its entire length. Aqueducts, listed buildings and several canal museums, as well as old mileposts and date plaques, make the Grand Union's towpath a fascinating route, which also passes through some outstanding scenic countryside.

The magnificent beech woods of the Chilterns have traditionally supplied the furniture-making industry in and around High Wycombe. There were once extensive forests across the region and timber was then also the primary construction material, as can be seen from surviving examples of medieval timber-framed houses in the older towns, such as Hertford and St Albans. Brick-making from local clay began in Tudor times; it gained momentum in the 18th century to overtake the timber industry, so brick now dominates townscapes. North of High Wycombe, near the old market town of Wendover, is Coombe Hill. At 832 ft (260 m) this is the highest point in the Chilterns, and the views from the summit stretch over 7 miles (11 km). This landmark is owned by the National Trust and crowned with a monument to local men who lost their lives in the Boer War. A couple of miles away stands Chequers, the official country residence of successive British Prime Ministers since 1917. The core of the building is thought to date from the 13th century.

The southern part of Buckinghamshire and Hertfordshire is rich agricultural land, mainly arable in the west and concentrating on horticulture in the east, where the land is fed by chalk stream tributaries of the River Lea on the Essex border. Perhaps surprisingly, in view of the post-war birth of new towns such as Welwyn Garden City and the accompanying rise of new industries, agriculture is still the chief source of income for the region. Still more remarkable is the fact that the biggest town in Hertfordshire (Watford) has a population of only 110,000 when this small county's total population approaches 1 million. Moreover, Hertford's population of 22,000 makes it one of the smallest county towns in England.

The noteworthy history of these shires is mainly recent and associated with achievements of individuals, although the older inheritances of the region may be seen in Roman St Albans (27) and Saxon Hertford (29), as well as along the Icknield Way (see page 5) whose exact age is unknown but which may well have its origins in the Neolithic Stone Age (3000–1800 BC). Buckinghamshire has been a breeding ground for top politicians since the mid 17th century, and has spawned no less than six Prime Ministers, the best known being Benjamin Disraeli, who lived at Hughenden Manor (23) and whose political achievements include significant widening of the electorate and consolidation of the Empire, culminating in Queen Victoria becoming Empress of India. Prior to this, Edmund Burke, the 18th-century statesman famous for his analysis of the emancipation question, also lived in Buckinghamshire.

Literary figures who have been drawn to the region over the last three centuries include Irish playwright George Bernard Shaw, who lived near Knebworth (also the ancestral home of 19th-century novelist and politician Edward Bulwer Lytton—see Walk 28), and essayist and author of Tales from Shakespeare for children, Charles Lamb, who lived near Widford (30) in the early 19th century. Lamb described the Hertfordshire countryside as 'homely and humpy', which presumably refers to the county's gentle charm in contrast to the more dramatic landscapes of other parts of the country.

The River Lea (also spelt Lee) acts as a natural boundary between Hertfordshire and Essex. It is straddled by Lee Valley Park, which stretches 23 miles (37 km) northward from East London and incorporates a 50-mile (80 km) Lee Valley Walk as well as a network of other walking trails and some important wetland wildlife habitats. Just above the M25 next to the River Lea stands Waltham Abbey, which was founded by Harold, the last Saxon king, who was reputedly buried there after he died at the hands of William the Conqueror at the Battle of Hastings.

The history of Waltham Abbey is one example of Essex's rich heritage which belies the county's reputation for a dearth of interesting history or culture. The landscapes of the county are also more attractive and varied than might be expected. Although the countryside of the north—the green fields, winding lanes and picturesque villages of Constable's best-known paintings—is on the whole most alluring, there are within closer range of London ancient woodlands, meadows and riverscapes, and wildlife rich estuaries approaching the coast.

As was the case in many parts of Britain, a large proportion of this region was once covered in woodland. Unusually, in Essex large tracts of ancient woodland (that is dating from at least the beginning of the first millenium AD, and possibly from the end of the last Ice Age) have survived: namely Epping *(31)*, Hatfield *(32)* and Hainault forests. In the Middle Ages Epping and Hainault were incorporated into Waltham Forest, which was a massive 60,000 acres (24,240 hectares) in total. In 1062 it was the subject of one of the earliest recorded charters documenting woodland. However, a 'forest' would not have been entirely wooded as the old definition of the term was a place where deer roamed—otherwise known as a 'chase', where the king and nobles hunted. This might have taken in parkland, heathland (now being reclaimed in Epping) and rides (as at Hatfield). William the Conqueror first introduced the concept of the 'king's deer' and thereafter the forests became crown land and the deer were fiercely protected from poachers. Queen Elizabeth's Hunting Lodge at Chingford within Epping Forest is the best preserved example of a Tudor hunting lodge in England.

Deer survive in the Essex forests due to careful intervention, though they are less likely to be seen here than in Windsor Great Park. Of the big three, only Hainault suffered systematic deforestation after royal interest had declined in the mid 19th century. Long distance walks in Essex include the 25-mile (40 km) Forest Way *(32)*, which links the forests of Epping and Hatfield, as well as the 81-mile (130 km) Essex Way *(33)* stretching from Epping Forest to the coast at Harwich. Afforestation across southern Essex is currently occurring through the Thames Chase community project, which is also extending areas of meadow, lakes, wetland and parkland. Essex County Council administers 12 country parks which contain a range of landscapes, from the ancient coppiced hornbeam woodlands of the Weald and Thorndon *(34)* parks near Brentwood to the pasture and salt marshes of Hadleigh Castle Country Park beside the Thames estuary *(35)*.

The late medieval castle at Hadleigh was once owned by Richard II and was later home to three of Henry VIII's wives: Katherine of Aragon, Anne of Cleves and Katherine Parr. The building was largely destroyed by landslides; Constable painted its ruins. Hadleigh and Rayleigh to the north were within the boundaries of a royal hunting park. There was an older castle at Rayleigh—the only one in Essex mentioned in the Domesday Book—but all that remains are the motte and baileys. Tilbury, to the south-west, was the scene of Elizabeth I's famous speech to the men about to engage in battle at sea with the Spanish Armada in 1588: 'I know I have the body of a weak and feeble woman, but I have the heart of a king.' The fort at Tilbury was built a century later to defend against a threatened Dutch invasion.

No longer occupied by royals or used strategically, the north bank of the Thames mouth and estuaries of the rivers Crouch and Blackwater are now important natural landscapes, where the rare and fragile ecosystem of the salt marshes and mud flats is preserved. In the Iron Age and later periods salt was extracted from the seaweed here, and the Saxons laid fish traps in the estuaries. In its more recent history, the eastern Thames provided for a thriving shrimping and cockling industry. Fishing and shellfish collecting, as well as boatbuilding, are still a source of income in the area.

Wildlife

Woodland   (2–16, 18, 22–24, 26–35)

In the diverse woods and forests around London, coniferous plantations nestle next to ancient broad-leaved forest, much of which bears the tell-tale hallmarks of medieval forest management —coppicing and pollarding (see *Walk 31* for a definition). Dominant tree species include the ancient oak, hornbeam, beech and silver birch, which provide a habitat (especially in the ancient forests) for many interesting fungi, lichens and insects.

Foxes, badgers and fallow deer, though rarely seen, are common residents in most of the woods around London. Fallow deer are present, for example, in the forests of Hatfield *(32)*, Epping *(31)* and the Weald Country Park in south-west Essex (but not Windsor). An introduced population of red deer is also widespread, and may be seen at Windsor. However, the red and roe deer are restricted to the south-west (Surrey and Berkshire, including Windsor Forest), while you may catch sight of a muntjac, a small introduced deer species, in the woods of Hertfordshire and Buckinghamshire as well as in Hatfield Forest, where there is also a herd of sika deer.

More prominent are woodland birds, which are found in profusion in all types of forest. Common sights (and sounds) in most forests include large flocks of tits (great, blue, coal and long-tailed) and green woodpeckers. At dusk and dawn the eerie cry of the tawny owl can be heard ringing out through broad-leaved woodland. In Hatfield forest, look out for the flashing colours of jays that swoop across paths. Less conspicuous, but equally entertaining, are the mottled brown treecreepers that forage along the trunks of old, gnarled trees.

In the Kentish woods you may see perfectly symmetrical holes gnawed in hazelnuts— evidence of the presence of one of the rarest British mammals, the shy nocturnal dormouse.

Downs and grasslands   (3, 8–12, 26)

The chalk grasslands of the North Downs are maintained by the constant grazing pressure of rabbits. Indeed, when myxamatosis decimated the rabbit population in the mid-fifties, serious encroachment of trees occurred in many places, the effects of which may still be seen today. Hills and downlands also support a rich diversity of plant life including, on the wooded Chiltern Hills, several rare orchids such as the bird's-nest orchid. During the summer, the downs literally teem with a diverse range of insects. For example, there are over 50 species of butterfly in the Chilterns, including the smallest British butterfly, the aptly named small blue. Thrushes and fieldfares forage alongside blackbirds and starlings in the summer, while kestrels, sparrowhawks and the occasional tawny owl may be seen hunting. Foxes and badgers are present, if rarely seen.

Wetlands and river valleys
(4, 6-21, 25, 27, 29, 30, 32-35)

Some of the largest and best kept lakes in southern England surround London, which are an important wildlife habitat. Wraysbury lakes, for example, support many fish and waterfowl, detailed in *Walk 17*. Look out for the rare fish-eating smew around lakes and ponds, and for the mandarin duck which was introduced to Virginia Waters in Surrey and has subsequently spread over large parts of south-east England. Another unusual visitor is the red-eared terrapin, many of which have escaped from captivity or been released to colonise ponds and canals throughout the south-east.

Near streams and river banks, look for kingfishers, herons and green woodpeckers as well as dragon-flies and damselflies (also seen around the edges of ponds, especially in forests and heathland). On the water, you will see swans, ducks, coots and moorhens. Plant life on river banks includes purple and yellow loosestrife, and in streams and ponds, waterlilies, bur-reeds and flowering rush. In the meadows and hedgerows, warblers and the occasional hobby may be seen in summer, whilst winter visitors include lapwings and snipe.

Parkland   (2, 5, 7, 28)

In the well-maintained parklands around London, foxes and badgers are commonly seen at dawn and dusk, and rabbits have reached such propor-tions that they may now be seen at any time of the day. In summer, many butterfly species may be seen both in the open parklands and the forest margins. One of the great attractions of parks is the opportunity to see clearly some of Britain's most characteristic bird species. Among the most impressive are the kestrel, often seen hovering over long grassland in search of small rodents, and the sparrowhawk. The parks to the south and west of London also provide a home to one of the most colourful immigrants, the ring-necked parakeet. Deer are also common in many parks, where they have been actively introduced (see *Woodland* section on page 8).

Heathland   (14)

Heathland in our area of study is concentrated mainly in Surrey, plus some areas in southern Hertfordshire and Essex. It ranges from the wet heath of Ockley Common *(14)* to more typical dry heath. Grasses, mosses and one of Britain's few predaceous plants, the sundew (which captures and digests insects on its sticky leaves), are abundant in the wetter areas, while pink and white heathers are characteristic of the sandy heaths. Common lizards and adders are abundant on most heaths and can often be seen sunning themselves on the edge of paths during the height of the summer. The heathland pools contain many species of dragonfly as well as palmate newts. Birds seen on the Surrey heaths include the exceedingly rare Dartford warbler, which has gradually spread east from Hampshire over the last five years. If you are out in the late evening, you could be lucky enough to see a nightjar. This rare summer migrant, although completely insectivorous, used to be known as a 'goat sucker' due to the hairs that surround its mouth.

The heath ecosystem is fragile and is regarded by many ecologists as a transitional community maintained by periodic fires. Consequently, in many heaths, such as Long Running within Epping Forest, there are signs of encroachment from purple moor grass and birch saplings, and active management occurs.

Estuaries (1, 35)

The estuaries east of London are home to many interesting plants and birds. As you get nearer the sea, you may even spot a common seal lounging on the mud flats. Salt marshes contain a number of interesting species of grass including the introduced weed, *Spartina*. Dunlins, curlews, oystercatchers and plovers are among 20,000 species of wading bird that winter on the Swale estuary alone. Brent geese, teal and mallards are also common.

Advice to Walkers

Clothing and equipment

The only essentials for all these walks are a pair of stout shoes or trainers (or wellingtons if it is likely to be wet or muddy) and an anorak, preferably with a hood. Any further requirements will depend on the type and length of walk you are undertaking, and the time of year. Make sure you wrap up well in the winter, and take gloves and a hat with you. It may not feel cold when you start out, but the wind can be bitter on the exposed downs. If you are a regular walker, it is worth investing in a pair of walking boots, which tend to be more comfortable than other footwear, especially on longer walks. It is also sensible to take a few carbohydrate-high snacks on longer walks, whether or not you plan to stop for a pub lunch. Be sure to take a bottle of water and a

sun-screen if you are walking in the open in summer. These items are most easily carried in a small rucksack, in which you could also put a basic first aid kit with plasters and some antiseptic cream.

In some cases, it may be desirable to take a sheet map and/or compass as well as this guidebook— see *Using the guidebook* below.

Getting there

Instructions on how to get to the start of each route by car and by public transport are given. For some of the walks, limited parking space rather than a car park is indicated. If you are driving, take care to park safely and considerately, making sure that you are not on private land or blocking access to property.

Using public transport reduces pressure on roads and therefore helps to safeguard the countryside from new road building. With the non-car owning city resident in mind, we have included a high proportion of walks directly accessible by rail from the main London stations. Others may be reached using a combination of train and bus. You are strongly urged to check public transport services in advance. Telephone numbers of county council travel information helplines are given on page 11. Some of the rail companies publish special ramblers' maps; it may be worth enquiring about these at your local station.

Using the guidebook

If you are unused to any exercise, start with one of the many short, easy routes. That said, grading differentials are not great and most moderately fit people could cope with the vast majority of walks in this book, if not all of them.

Navigation is more likely to pose a problem, as few of the walks are conducted wholly on broad expanses of open land where landmarks are visible. They tend to involve a number of cross-overs from one footpath to another, which can be especially confusing when there are a large number of public paths in the area. You will reduce the likelihood of going astray if you pay attention to both the text and map at each stage. Where the introductory text warns of potential problems, it may be wise to take a sheet map or even a compass as precautionary back-up. Rights of way are marked on the Ordnance Survey's Pathfinder and Explorer maps, which are both at the scale of 2.5 inches to one mile (4 cm to 1 km) or 1:25,000. It is safer to allow the maximum, not the minimum time you think it will take to complete the route.

Country roads are not immune to the dangers of traffic. Be careful when crossing main roads and take care too on narrow and windy country lanes, where drivers do not always anticipate pedestrians and sometimes charge around corners.

Rights of Way and the Country Code

Public footpaths are legal Rights of Way, which means that where they exist the landowner may not object to people walking on his land, provided they follow a few simple rules which are summarised by the Country Code below. If you are walking a dog, it is imperative that you do not allow it to worry livestock. When crossing land where animals are grazed, always keep your dog on a lead. If it causes a nuisance, you are liable for prosecution and the dog may legally be shot! Farmers do occasionally put obstructions across legitimate paths. Please report any obstructions you may find to the county council's highway authority. If the farmer has ploughed over the path, you may still walk where the path should have been. The Country Code is:

Enjoy the countryside and respect its life and work.

Guard against all risk of fire.

Fasten all gates.

Keep your dogs under close control.

Keep to public paths across farmland.

Use gates and stiles to cross fences, hedges and walls.

Leave livestock, crops and machinery alone.

Take your litter home.

Help to keep all water clean.

Protect wildlife, plants and trees.

Take special care on country roads.

Make no unnecessary noise.

Detailed information about your rights and responsibilities in the countryside is given in the Countryside Commission's booklet *Out in the Country*.

Useful Contacts

The British Rail telephone enquiry lines and talking timetable numbers for each region are set out on a display page in the BT phone book. Information regarding trains serving walks in this book was kindly supplied by South West Trains, Network South Central, South Eastern, Thames Trains, Chiltern Railways and West Anglia Great Northern (WAGN).

Local bus information and journey planning advice (including rail connections) may be obtained by ringing the following county council operated services:

Kent traveline: 0800 696996
Surrey traveline: 01737 223000
Buckinghamshire traveline: 0345 328000
Hertfordshire traveline: 0345 244344
Essex bus line (buses only): 0345 000333

If you want to combine your walk with some sightseeing, contact the local tourist information centre to find out about attractions in the area. The English Tourist Board should be able to put you in touch with the appropriate local office:

English Tourist Board
Thames Tower
Black's Road
London W6 9EL
Tel 0181-846 9000

Other useful addresses are:

Countryside Commission
John Dower House
Crescent Place
Cheltenham
Gloucestershire GL50 3RA

National Rivers Authority
Rivers House
Waterside Drive
Aztec West
Almondsbury
Bristol BS12 4UD

National Trust
36 Queen Anne's Gate
London SW1H 9AS

Walk 1
RIVERSIDE COUNTRY PARK

5 miles (8 km) there and back   Easy

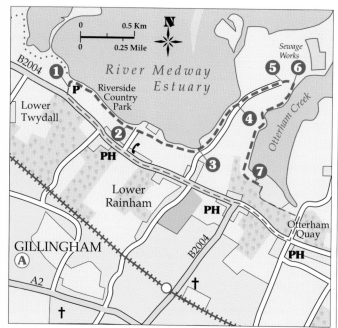

⑤ Just before the entrance to the sewage works there is a stile over a fence to the right (signposted). Cross this and continue by the side of the fence.

⑥ Cross the footbridge over a small ditch and climb up onto the sea wall beyond. Turn right along this, with Otterham Creek down to the left.

⑦ At this point the path reaches the edge of an industrial complex. Either return by the same route or else skirt around the edge of the complex until it joins the public road and return that way (see route map). The first option provides the more pleasant walking and avoids the traffic .

Point of interest

Ⓐ Gillingham is a relatively modern arm of the conurbation clustered around the head of the Medway Estuary. While in the area it is worth visiting the naval dockyard in neighbouring Chatham—three miles (5 km) west of the start of the walk—and the town centre of Rochester, two miles (3 km) beyond. Chatham began its long association with the Royal Navy when a repair yard was founded there in 1547. In the following centuries it developed into a dockyard, and attracted visitors such as Pepys, Peter the Great (a keen boatbuilder himself) and Nelson (the *Victory* was built here). The dockyard exhibits cover an 80-acre (32 hectares) site. The attractions of Rochester include the cathedral (originally 11th century, but with additions up to the 14th century), the enormous ruined keep of Rochester Castle (11th/12th centuries) and the Charles Dickens Centre.

A flat, linear, coastal route, following the edge of the mud flats which surround the broad estuary of the River Medway. The route follows clear tracks and footpaths, with a possible return by public road (this can be quite a busy road, so considerable caution should be observed). To reach the start of the route, leave the M25 at junction 2 and take the A2 to the edge of Rochester. Continue through the town and over the Medway bridge to Chatham, then go north along the B2004 which bears west beside the estuary. Three miles (5 km) on, park in the large car park behind the dunes. PUBLIC TRANSPORT: There are frequent trains from London Victoria to Rainham, but bus 131 from Rainham station only passes the park twice daily (Mon-Fri) in each direction.

Route description

① Walk from the car park onto the track running along the edge of the estuary. Ahead and to the left is the headland of Horrid Hill, and a shore path continues beyond that for those who wish to explore it. For this route, turn right.

② Go past the breakers yard and continue along the shore beyond.

③ Swing to the left along the top of a dyke, with a small public road down to the right.

④ When the shore swings to the left carry on along the road.

Walk 2
SHORNE WOOD COUNTRY PARK   8 miles (13 km)   Moderate/Difficult

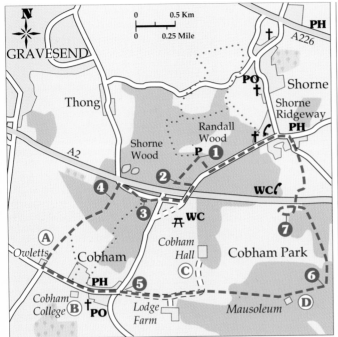

❸ At the split in the path keep right, then follow the path back onto the road for a short distance before turning left at the next arrow, back into the wood.

❹ The paths through the wood are numerous. Continue walking to the south-west until the village of Cobham is reached. Turn left along the road.

❺ At the junction at the eastern end of the village carry straight on along a clear track. When a road cuts right into Lodge Farm continue straight ahead, and when the main track turns left into Cobham Hall continue along a rougher path.

❻ Beyond the Mausoleum look for the path which cuts left back down to the road, passing to the left of Knights Place.

❼ Cross the A2 on a small bridge and continue beyond up to Shorne Ridgeway. Turn left along the public road, then left at the junction, to return to the car park.

Points of interest

Ⓐ Owletts is a red-brick Kentish farmhouse, built in 1683-4. It is open to the public Apr-Sep 14.00-17.00 on Wed and Thur.

Ⓑ The church dates in part from the mid 13th century. Behind it is the site of Cobham College, founded in 1362 by Sir John de Cobham. The buildings were later converted into almshouses .

Ⓒ The red-brick Cobham Hall is essentially late Elizabethan, with a central block dating from the mid 17th century. The landscaping was the work of Humphrey Repton in the late 18th century. The Hall now houses a school.

Ⓓ The Mausoleum was built for the 3rd Earl of Darnley in 1783, but was never used.

This circuit is one of a number of possible signposted routes which begin from the Shorne Wood Country Park (a leaflet is available at the park). The route can be tricky to follow in the densely wooded sections, but it is difficult to go too far wrong. Features of this particular route include the village of Cobham and a distant view of Cobham Hall. Parts of the route follow public roads: due care should be taken on these sections. To reach the park, leave the M25 at junction 2 and take the A2 past Gravesend. Turn off towards Shorne and a short distance along the road, park in the Shorne Wood car park on the left. PUBLIC TRANSPORT: There are frequent trains from London Charing Cross to Gravesend. From there, buses 222 and 310 (on Sat) go infrequently along the A2.

Route description

❶ From the main car park walk south (ie towards the A2) following the signs for the Woodland Car Park.

❷ Follow the track to the road bridge over the main road. On the far side of the road drop down to the left, then double back beneath the bridge. Follow a road running parallel to the A2. At the junction with a second road, look for the yellow arrow marking the start of a path through the woods opposite.

13

Walk 3
HOLLY HILL

**5 miles (5 km)   Easy/Moderate;
strenuous between ❼ and ❽**

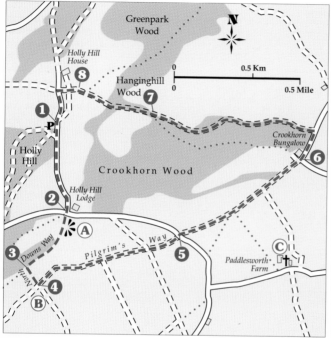

❸ Cross the first stile and bear left, continuing on the North Downs Way, down the field to the next junction.

❹ Turn left at the crossroads and proceed along the well-worn footpath (Pilgrim's Way) between the hedges. Follow the path for three-quarters of a mile (1.2 km) until reaching the road.

❺ Bear left at the road, then immediately turn right and continue following the Pilgrim's Way for a further three-quarters of a mile (1.2 km), straight ahead until emerging at a concrete road.

❻ Bear left (but ignore the path into the woods behind the bungalow). Take the left-hand footpath (FP47) which leads along the northern edge of Crookhorn Wood. (The path is well-defined most of the way, but may confuse where an arm of Crookhorn Wood juts into a field on the right. Bear gently left here then, after two or three minutes, bear right to continue along the northern edge of the wood.)

❼ At the end of the field on the right, the fence extends into the wood beside the path and another path joins from the left. Proceed straight ahead, on the steep uphill path between rows of silver birch and beech trees. At the top of the hill, cross over the stile and continue straight ahead on the path between two fields (beneath some large ash trees).

❽ At the top of the fields, go straight across the private drive (leading to Holly Hill House). A few steps on, the path meets the road. Turn left and follow the road for a quarter of a mile (0.4 km) until reaching Holly Hill car park where the walk began.

A route that uses two historic paths, on the hillside at the top of the North Downs escarpment and across farmland. To reach the start of the route, leave the M25 at junction 3 and join the M20. Come off at junction 4 and drive north on the A228. At the roundabout at the edge of Snodland, take the first left turn and at the T-junction turn left again into Snodland Road. Just over a mile (1.6 km) on, turn right into Stangate Road (signposted to Harvel and Meopham) and proceed for 2 miles (3.2 km) to the top of Holly Hill. Turn right up the lane beside Holly Hill Lodge and drive a short distance to the car park on the left. PUBLIC TRANSPORT: Not directly accessible. The nearest bus stop is at Vigo, a village nearly 2 miles (3 km) west of ❷ along White Horse Road. (Take a train from London Victoria to Meopham, then one of the regular buses to Vigo.)

Route description

❶ Facing the lane from the car park, turn right and proceed back down the lane to the T-junction.

❷ Cross the road, climb over the stile on the far side and continue down the bank, following the North Downs Way. (After a few steps, the path becomes more clearly defined and leads straight downhill beside the right-hand edge of a row of bushes.) At the bottom of the hill follow the path around to the right and along the lower edge of the woods.

Points of interest

(A) Extensive views can be enjoyed from this section of the path, over the Vale of Holmesdale and the Medway Valley. To the east, beyond the Medway Valley, the chalk escarpment of the North Downs extends far into the distance, dominating the landscape.

(B) At ❹ two long-distance footpaths diverge, having followed the same route west of our walk. The 120-mile (190 km) Pilgrim's Way is so named because medieval pilgrims used this track to travel from Winchester to Canterbury. The North Downs Way is 141 miles (227 km) long and runs from Farnham (in Surrey) to Dover. It is interesting to note the many species of tree and shrub that have colonised the hedges either side of the ancient Pilgrim's Way. Oak, ash, field maple, sycamore and whitebeam are a few of the trees present, while guelder rose, dog rose, dog wood and spindle are established in the shrub layer. In addition, ivy and clematis (traveller's joy) climb over everything within reach.

(C) Hidden amongst the buildings of Paddlesworth Farm is the tiny St Benedict's Church. The church lost most of its congregation and was abandoned during the Black Death. From 1678 until it was restored in 1930, it was used as a barn. Paddlesworth church now belongs to the Redundant Churches Fund and is preserved as an outstanding example of Norman architecture. A service is held there annually, on the first Sunday in October.

Walk 4

HOLLINGBOURNE CHURCH
TO LEEDS CASTLE

5 miles (8 km)
Easy; busy main road to cross

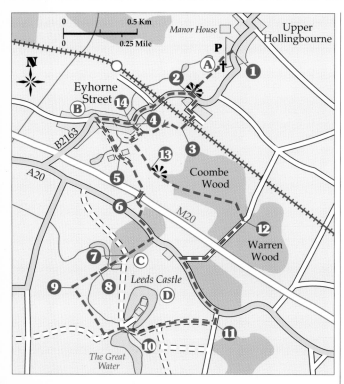

A relatively undemanding route that packs in a wealth of interesting features, varied scenery and great views; the chief attraction being the fairy-tale Leeds Castle. To reach the start of the route, leave the M25 at junction 3 and take the M20 past Maidstone to junction 8. Then drive north along the B2163 towards Sittingbourne. On entering Hollingbourne, continue across the railway track to the upper village and park by the church. PUBLIC TRANSPORT: Trains run direct from London Charing Cross or Victoria to Hollingbourne.

Route description

1 Begin the walk by following the path through the churchyard (to the right of All Saints Church) and continue along the straight path across the field beyond.

2 Turn left at the road and pro-ceed a short distance, then turn right into Culpepper Close (beside the telephone box). Follow the road around to the left, then take the first right turn onto a track which passes under the railway.

3 Follow the right-hand edge of the field and cross the little bridge and stile in the bottom right corner. Continue diagonally across the next field, aiming for the left-hand edge of the houses. Cross the stile beside the gate and proceed ahead along the cyprus-lined driveway to the road.

4 Turn left and follow the main road to The Windmill pub. At the far side of the pub, turn left and fol-low the lane past the village hall. Turn left at the farm buildings to skirt around the hay barn.

5 From the metal gate, follow the track ahead and around a bend to the left, leading along the top of a field. Continue into the next field, then bear right towards the motor-way footbridge. Aim for the exit point 20 yards from the far end of the field, where a path between wooden fences leads up to the bridge. Cross the bridge and follow the path down into the field.

6 Walk a few steps across the cor-ner of the field and climb over the stile into the trees. Follow the wood-land path to the road (the A20), then turn left. Proceed along the pave-ment for a short distance. Just over the hill and before reaching Park Gate Inn, cross the road (take care—it is very busy!). On the far side, follow the footpath leading through a gate.

7 Cross over the drive leading to Leeds Castle and proceed downhill beneath the beech trees. Walk straight past the lake, proceed beneath the large cedar tree and cross the stile at the end of the path.

8 Follow the path up the field to the yellow post (look for stones set into the ground beside the post). Proceed in a straight line along the top of the field as far as the gate to the cricket pitch.

9 Do not pass through the gate, but walk back into the present field, directly away from the gate. Proceed between the young trees to the next yellow post, then down the field to yet another yellow post. Continue along the private road until reaching Leeds Castle.

10 Turn right at the castle, then take the first left turn and follow the drive that gradually leads away from the castle, past the golf course to the road. (If the main gate onto the road is closed, follow the footpath downhill to the left, then turn right and follow the path uphill to the small metal gate.)

11 Turn left and proceed a short distance to the main road. Cross over and turn left to follow the path along the edge of the road towards Hollingbourne. Proceed for a third of a mile (0.5 km), then take the first right turn. Follow the lane uphill (it is quite steep for a short way), under the motorway bridge and onward.

12 Pass a cottage on the left and 20 yards on turn left along a narrow footpath leading into ancient woodland. Cross over the stile and proceed for a few minutes, bearing left at the large oak tree. Continue until the woodland clears on the left; climb over the stile into the left-hand field and follow its upper edge. Ignore the gate on the right at the end of Coombe Wood and continue to the end of the field.

13 Climb over the stile and proceed down the right-hand edge of the next field (the same one that was crossed in the other direction at **5**). Cross over the partially grown-in stile in the corner and continue straight ahead across the next field, aiming towards the tiled roof. Cross the stile in the corner at the far end of this field and follow the enclosed path to the right. Turn left along the gravel drive and proceed to the road.

14 Turn right and walk along the pavement for a few minutes. Continue beyond the railway bridge and turn left at the war memorial, then retrace your steps along the footpath back to Hollingbourne church.

Points of interest

A All Saints Church in Upper Hollingbourne occupies a superb position at the foot of the North Downs escarpment. It is an attractive medieval building, much restored in the 19th and 20th centuries, which contains memorials to the Culpepper family, 17th-century owners of nearby Hollingbourne Manor. The church's most treasured possession is an altar cloth ornamented with cherubs and fruits, made by Lady Elizabeth Culpepper's four daughters, which is kept locked away except during festivals.

B Eyhorne Street is a picturesque group of houses in a number of architectural styles dating from the 16th-century onwards. The early 15th-century Eyhorne Manor has been carefully restored by its present owner.

C A fine collection of British and exotic waterfowl may be viewed from the path.

D Leeds Castle is built upon two islands in a lake formed by the River Len, a tributary of the Medway. It is one of the most enchanting castles in Europe. The Saxons built a wooden fortress on the site in 857 AD, which was reconstructed in stone by the Normans, and the castle has been enlarged and altered through successive centuries. (Many of the defences, of medieval appearance, were put up in the 19th century.) In the late 13th century, Leeds Castle passed into the hands of the Royal Family and it remained in their possession for 300 years. The castle was later owned by various wealthy landowners, including the Culpepper family. It was refurbished to its present splendour by Lady Baillie, who acquired the castle in 1926, and was bequeathed to the nation when she died. Leeds Castle is open to the public from 11.00 daily, closing at 17.00 Mar-Oct and 15.00 Nov-Feb (the grounds open at 10.00).

Walk 5
KNOLE PARK

7 miles (11 km)   Moderate

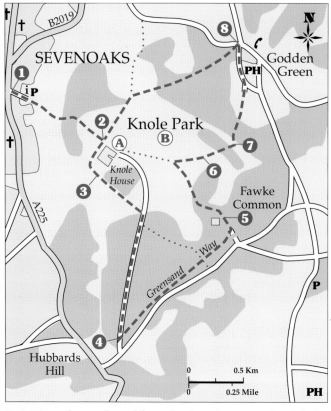

A circuit on clear tracks and footpaths through an area of undulating parkland heavily populated by fallow deer. Features of the route include Knole House and the little village of Godden Green. The route starts in Sevenoaks, which is easily reached by car from south-east London via the A21 or A224. There are extensive parking facilities near the town centre. PUBLIC TRANSPORT: Take the direct train to Sevenoaks from London Charing Cross.

Route description

❶ Turn off Sevenoaks High Street, following the signs for the Tourist Information Centre. Cross the car park beyond to join a footpath which leads down to a gate leading into Knole Park. Follow the rough path beyond: across a grassy swale and onto a low hill from which Knole House is visible.

❷ Turn right along the face of the house, and continue until the end of the walled garden. Turn left at the corner and continue beside the wall.

❸ When the wall ends carry straight on, through open parkland,

until the track joins a surfaced road. Turn right along this and follow it until it nears the road at the southern end of the park.

❹ Turn onto the major track joining from the left and continue along it until it ends at a T-junction. Turn left.

❺ Follow this track past a house, then on up the slope beyond (NB: be careful while crossing the golf course at this point). When the track approaches its highest point, look out for a grassy path doubling back to the right. Turn right onto this and follow it across a small valley.

❻ After climbing the far side of the valley the path crosses another grass track and then disappears. Look for a further rough path which starts a little beyond this point; it gradually becomes clearer as it leads down to the left of a stand of conifers, and then on to join a clear track beyond.

❼ Swing left past the houses and continue until the track reaches a T-junction. Turn left and continue until a further T-junction is reached.

❽ At this point a short detour to the right leads into the village of Godden Green. Alternatively, turn left and follow the clear track back to Knole House. Retrace your steps from there back to the car park.

Points of interest

Ⓐ Knole House was begun in 1456 and was the property of successive Archbishops of Canterbury until 1532, when it was commandeered by Henry VIII. Elizabeth I passed it on to Thomas Sackville, first Earl of Dorset, who extended and improved the building. The house is preserved intact outside and within and is open to the public Apr-Oct Wed-Sun and Bank hol Mon.

Ⓑ Knole Park comprises 1000 acres (404 hectares) of rolling parkland and woodland. A feature of the park is the large number of fallow deer.

18

Walk 6

GROOMBRIDGE AND HARRISON'S ROCKS

4 miles (6.5 km)

Moderate with some steep sections

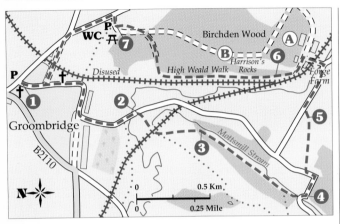

This route, on the Kent/Sussex border in the High Weald, takes in many interesting features unique to this beautiful area. To reach the start of the route, leave the M25 at junction 5 and take the A21 to Tonbridge, then the A26 into Tunbridge Wells town centre. Take the A264 west for 2 miles (3.2 km), then turn left along the B2110 to Groombridge. In the village, bear left at the mini-roundabout and park a short way on in a small car park on the left. PUBLIC TRANSPORT: Take a train from London Charing Cross to Tunbridge Wells, then bus 290 to Groombridge (Mon-Sat only in winter).

Route description

1 Cross the road from the car park and walk up the residential street ahead. Continue past St Thomas's Church (keeping to the pavement which runs along most of this stretch) and follow the road around to the right, then downhill to the left and past a sewage plant.

2 Cross the bridge over the stream, then immediately climb over the stile on your right (marked 'Sussex Border Path') and follow the path across the field and under the railway bridge. Take the left fork across the next field and proceed over the stile into the woods ahead.

3 Go over the next stile into a long, narrow field and walk ahead along the top of the field. At the far end, follow the narrow path into the woods. At the signpost, take the left fork and proceed to the road.

4 Turn left along the road, up a steep hill and onward. Soon after a sharp bend to the left, look out for a small gate into a field on the right, with a yellow arrow (just past a private driveway). Walk diagonally across the field towards the oast-house visible over the trees in the distance.

5 Cross the stile at the end of the field and cut down to the lane. Turn right and proceed for 200 yards, then turn into a driveway on the left (listen for the nearby waterfall). Cross over a stream and a railway track, turn left at the T-junction and go into the trees ahead.

6 On emerging into a field, proceed along the path beside the disused railway track. At the end of the second field, bear away from the railway track to a wood. Proceed up to the junction and cross straight over it onto a rougher path which continues fairly steeply uphill to the road.

7 Turn right along the private road to the junction, then left towards the village, bearing left at the fork. Almost immediately, turn left along an unmarked track, behind some houses and over the railway track. Bear left to the residential road on which the walk began and retrace your steps downhill, back to the start.

Points of interest

A Among the pretty group of cottages and farm buildings occupying this idyllic setting is a converted oasthouse—a characteristic feature of this part of rural England (see introduction, page 4).

B Harrison's Rocks, one of several natural outcrops of sandstone rocks in the area, are owned by the British Mountaineering Council. They reach up to 40 ft (12 m) high and have been used as a training ground by 11 Everest climbers.

Walk 7
PENSHURST

4 miles (6.5 km)   Moderate

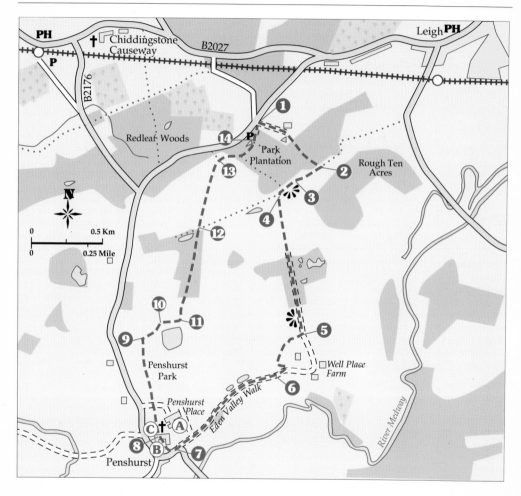

A pleasant walk through parkland and pockets of mixed woodland in the tranquil valley between the Rivers Eden and Medway, including some fine views. Expect to observe nature undisturbed (including dozens of rabbits). To reach the start of the route, leave the M25 at junction 5. Take the A21 bound for Tonbridge, then at the second junction turn onto the B245. Turn right into the B2027 for Leigh and, coming out of Leigh, take the left fork which crosses over the railway track. Just prior to a turn-off on the right, there is limited parking space in a lay-by. PUBLIC TRANSPORT: Trains run regularly from Charing Cross to Tonbridge, where you can change for Leigh or Penshurst (Penshurst station is at Chiddingstone Causeway). If coming from Leigh station, start from ❷.

Route description

❶ Take the footpath beside the lay-by, up into Penshurst Estate. Continue past a farm and down into the woods.

❷ Cross the stile where the woods end and turn sharp right. Walk diagonally across the field, up to another stile and gate in the corner. (On this stile is a yellow arrow marked 'Eden Valley Walk: link path'.)

❸ Cross the stile and walk straight ahead.

❹ A short way along the broad grassy path, turn left (you will see Penshurst Place in the distance) and go down the edge of a cultivated field. Go over the stile into woods, then over another stile and along a tree-lined avenue. Continue until you reach an unmarked gate (without a stile and with buildings beyond).

❺ This side of the gate, turn right down the edge of the field. Cross the stile in the corner and walk along the edge of the next field for about 30 yards, until a stile to the left takes you onto a surfaced drive.

❻ Turn right, passing two ponds. Continue up to Penshurst Place and pass by, leaving the house on your right. At the end of the boundary wall, exit through a brick archway extending from the old gatehouse.

❼ Turn right, up towards the village, and right again almost immediately into an old courtyard ('Leicester Square'). Pass under a beam into the churchyard and walk around the church.

❽ Behind the church, the walk continues over a stile and back across the field, this time on the left of Penshurst Place. Go straight across the lane via stiles and walk through parkland, leaving a cricket pitch to your right.

❾ When level with the large pond on the right, bear right towards a stile in the fence ahead.

❿ Once over the stile, turn right along the bottom of the field and past the pond.

⓫ Guided by a series of 'V' shaped stiles marked with yellow arrows, go diagonally up across another field, and climb the hill on the path through the trees.

⓬ At the top of the hill, go straight ahead (across converging paths) down a gentle slope with saplings on either side.

⓭ On reaching mature woodland, turn right and walk along the edge of the woods. Turn left at the crossroads, up a furrowed path through the trees.

⓮ As the woods open out, the path joins another one. Bear left and walk down to the road where you started.

Points of interest

Ⓐ Penshurst Place dates from medieval times. Intact at its heart is a 14th-century manor built by a wealthy merchant banker. This incorporates the magnificent Great Hall—with a 60 ft high chestnut roof—where Henry VIII was entertained by the Duke of Buckingham. Penshurst Place is currently owned by William Sidney, Viscount de L'Isle, to whose ancestors the house was given by Edward VI in 1552. The Italianate formal gardens at Penshurst are as old as the original building, although most features were created in the 16th and 17th centuries. Both the house and gardens are open to the public daily Apr-Sep and at weekends in Mar and Oct (house 12.00-17.30; gardens 11.00-18.00). Telephone (01892) 870307 for details.

Ⓑ Leicester Square is a small picturesque courtyard partly enclosed by a group of 16th-century houses. The square was named after the then Earl of Leicester, Robert Sidney, who also owned London's more famous Leicester Square.

Ⓒ Passing under a beam at the end of Leicester Square, one enters the graveyard of the sandstone Church of St John the Baptist. Thomas Becket appointed the first church warden in the 12th century and he is commemorated in the beautiful Becket Window designed by Penshurst resident and well-known artist Lawrence Lee. The adjoining Sidney Chapel contains a history of the family since the 16th century.

Walk 8
CHEVENING AND DISTRICT   4.5 miles (7 km)   Moderate/Strenuous

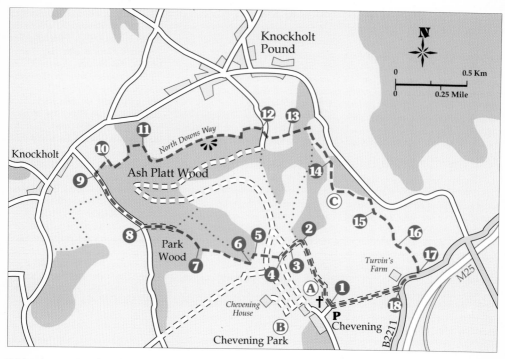

Taking in over 2 miles of the North Downs Way, this walk offers some magnificent views across the Kent countryside and of an imposing royal residence. To reach the start of the route, exit the M25 at junction 4; take the A224 south, parallel to the motorway, and continue for about 4 miles (6.4 km). Get onto Sundridge Road (B2211) at the roundabout, then take the first right into Chevening. Park in the car park behind the church. PUBLIC TRANSPORT: Take a train from London Charing Cross to Knockholt station, then bus 402 to Knockholt Pound. Start the walk at ⑫. Trains and buses run Mon-Sat only.

Route description

❶ Begin the walk behind St Botolph's Church. Pass through the gate on the northern edge of the churchyard and proceed straight along the footpath.

❷ A third of a mile (0.5 km) on, cross the first stile on the left. Continue along the left-hand side of the field.

❸ Cross the next two stiles either side of a private road and continue for a short distance beside the wood.

❹ Ignoring the stile in the corner of the field, turn right and follow the left-hand edge of the field. Continue past the water trough, across the next private road and up the farm track towards the wood.

❺ Turn left, pass through the metal gate and follow the track along the edge of the wood.

❻ Pass through the next metal kissing gate and turn right. Proceed beside the wood to the top of the hill.

❼ Continue straight ahead along the woodland track (still slightly uphill), then ignore the right-hand turn and proceed along the main track through Park Wood.

❽ At the end of the track, turn right by Keepers Cottage and follow the road for half a mile.

22

9 Cross the stile on the right, at the end of the woodland. Walk along the right-hand edge of the field, following the North Downs Way.

10 Cross the stile at the far side of the field. Walk a few steps along the woodland track then turn left to continue along the straight path at the top edge of Ash Platt wood.

11 Cross the stile at the end of the woodland path and turn right. Walk close to the woodland edge until eventually arriving at the road.

12 Turn right along the private road, then almost immediately turn left to continue following the North Downs Way along the top edge of the field.

13 Cross the stile in the corner. Follow the path between the private woods, cross the next stile, turn right and follow the outside edge of the wood.

14 When the woodland edge turns sharp right, proceed straight ahead. Cross the stile in the corner of the field and turn left to follow the top edge of the next field.

15 Cross the stile in the corner again, beside the wood. Proceed along the left-hand edge of the next field, still following the North Downs Way. The path soon bears right and drops downhill beside a hedge.

16 At the bottom, pass through a rough hedge, then follow the left-hand edge of the field to meet the road.

17 Turn right and follow the road to the bend just beyond Turvin's Farm.

18 When the road bears left, proceed almost straight ahead along the public footpath between Turvin's Farm and a roadside cottage. Follow the path in a straight line, back to St Botolph's Church.

Points of interest

A St Botolph's Church dates from the 13th century, with a battlemented tower added during the 16th century. Many interesting monuments are housed inside, including tombs of the Lennard and Stanhope families who were successive owners of Chevening House.

B A good view of Chevening House can be obtained from the village. There are also more distant views through a narrow gap in the trees between **11** and **12**, and from a vantage point between **14** and **15**. The house was built in the early 17th century in the style of Inigo Jones, and remodelled during the 18th century. In 1959 the 7th Earl of Stanhope gave the estate to the nation. It was his wish that, following his death, the house be used by a Cabinet Minister or member of the Royal Family. Prince Charles subsequently lived at Chevening House during his bachelor days.

C Good views can be obtained in all directions from this point: Chevening House and St Botolph's Church are on the right, and Sevenoaks is on the left—famous for its public school and for Knole, one of the largest stately homes in England.

Walk 9
FARTHING DOWNS

3 or 6 miles (5 or 9.5 km) Moderate

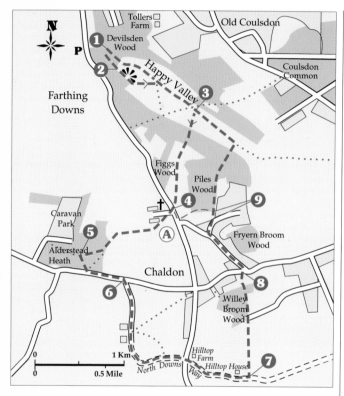

A signposted circuit across a chalk ridge and through farmland and woods. Two alternative routes (described on a notice-board at the start) use some of the numerous paths in the area straddling the Greater London border to the south of Coulsdon. To reach the start of the route, drive south into Coulsdon on the A23, then turn left onto Marlpit Lane (for Caterham) and take the second turning to the right, into Downs Road. Follow this road to the large car park at the far end of the ridge. PUBLIC TRANSPORT: Take the Brighton train from London Victoria to Coulsdon South.

Route description

1 Go into woodland, down the track leading off from the little pavilion containing the notice-board.

2 On emerging from the woods, follow the path down across the field, then bend left to walk along the valley floor.

3 Take the second turn to the right, uphill again across the field, then through a band of trees and over cultivated farmland until emerging onto the road, opposite the church.

At this point a short-cut may be taken which by-passes stages **4** – **8**, thereby halving the length of the walk. If following this option, turn left and walk a short way along the road towards Chalden, then turn left onto a clear path which leads past Piles Wood to rejoin the main route at **9**.

4 Cross the road and take the footpath to the left of the church lane.

5 Once on the heath, take a sharp left turn towards the lane, then walk left along the lane until you reach a junction.

6 Turn off to the right and follow the road as it narrows to a track then becomes a lane again, bending around to the left.

7 Continue past Hilltop Farm, and later Hilltop House, then turn onto a track to the left and follow it into some woods. Go straight through the woods until you emerge onto Rook Lane.

8 Cross the road and walk up Doctors Lane, then bear right into Leazes Avenue.

9 Turn left into the woods, then left again after emerging into the valley. Follow the path along the central track on the valley floor, which will lead you back to the start.

Point of interest

Ⓐ St Peter and St Paul's Church, parts of which date from the 12th century, contains a rare and grotesque medieval mural of Heaven, Hell and Purgatory. This was rediscovered in 1870 beneath several coats of whitewash.

Walk 10
JUNIPER BOTTOM TO BOX HILL 2 miles (3 km) Easy; sometimes muddy

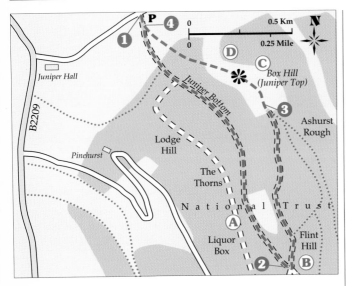

appreciated.) Proceed just a few more steps to reach the car park.

Points of interest

(A) Notice the abundant yew trees on the steep sides of the valley. Box trees/bushes proliferate near the top of the hill.

(B) An amazing variety of trees—including beech, oak, yew, birch, holly and box—are present in these woods. They support a wide range of birds, including woodpeckers, nuthatches, long-tailed tits and the much rarer marsh tit. Summer visiting birds include the willow warbler, chiffchaff, garden warbler and blackcap.

(C) Juniper Hall is tucked into the bottom of the valley on the left, with Norbury Park woodlands forming a backdrop beyond. Now owned by the National Trust and used as a field study centre, Juniper Hall was built in the 18th century and was for a time the home of a distinguished group of French aristocrats, including Tallyrand and Madame de Staël, who had flown the French Revolution.

(D) The open chalk downland is covered in a profusion of delightful flowers during the summer months. The rich flora, including several species of orchid (never to be picked), support many species of butterfly and other interesting insects. Green woodpeckers may be seen attacking ants' nests on the ground, and it is possible that you will glimpse a sparrowhawk swooping along the woodland edge in search of warblers. Most of the mammal species present on the downs are elusive or nocturnal, but grey squirrels and roe deer are fairly common and are often encountered during the day.

A short walk through National Trust owned countryside on the quieter north-facing side of Box Hill. There is much here of interest to the natural history enthusiast, both in the woods and on the downs. To reach the start of the route, drive south from Leatherhead (exit M25 at junction 9) on the A24. About 3 miles (4.8 km) on, turn left at the third roundabout, following the sign to Mickleham and Box Hill. Half a mile (0.8 km) on, turn left just beyond Juniper Hill House. At the end of the wall on your right, park (limited space) underneath the trees next to the Box Hill sign. Take care not to obstruct gateways. PUBLIC TRANSPORT: Take the Horsham train from London Victoria to Leatherhead, then London & Country bus 465 from Leatherhead bus station towards Dorking.

Route description

❶ Follow the track leading away from the road and proceed straight ahead along the bottom of the dry valley (Juniper Bottom). Continue along the valley for nearly a mile (1.6 km) until reaching the major junction of paths at the top.

❷ Turn left at the junction. (There is a large yew tree at its centre.) Follow the track between the trees, then fork left at the divide (along the more obvious route). Proceed underneath some fine beech trees and past the 'No Horses' sign.

❸ Pass through the kissing gate at the end of the path and continue onto the open downland. Aim to proceed down the open hillside, keeping to the crest of the ridge.

❹ Continue to the bottom of the hill and pass through the kissing gate. (There is a National Trust collection box here—donations are

Walk 11
LEITH HILL

6 miles (9.5 km)   Moderate/Difficult

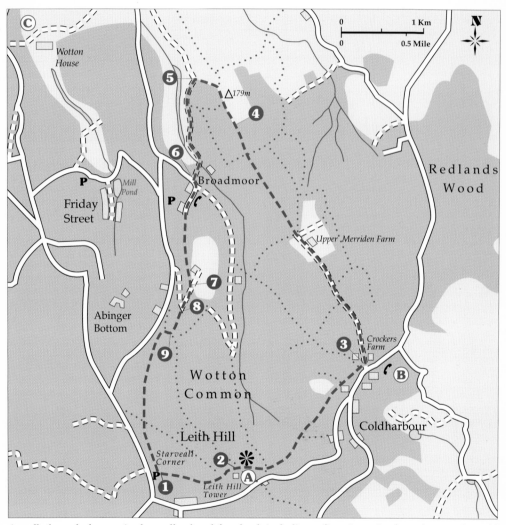

A walk through dense mixed woodland and farmland, including a fine viewpoint from the top of an old folly. Due to the proliferation of paths in the woods, it is recommended that a detailed area map is used. The start of the route is about 6 miles (9.7 km) south-west of Dorking. Take the A24 (exit 9 from the M25) to the outskirts of Dorking, then go west on the A25 until you reach Wotton village. Turn left into Sheephouse Lane, which is signposted for Leith Hill. Three miles (5 km) along, park in the large car park at Starveall Corner. PUBLIC TRANSPORT: Take the Horsham train from London Victoria to Dorking, then London & Country nostalgia bus 433 to Coldharbour (Sun and Bank hols only; no winter service).

Route description

1 From the back of the car park, follow the sign for Leith Tower. The footpath leads through mixed woodland for just under a mile (1.5 km) up to the tower.

2 Continue past the tower, down a steep slope, across a track at the bottom, then up the other side and on along the main track to Coldharbour, passing the cricket ground on the way.

3 From the village, turn left up the track signposted as a footpath to Buryhill Woods. Go straight along it for about 2 miles (3 km), first through woods, then passing Upper Merriden Farm and back into woods.

4 Note a field and a trig point on the right, and soon afterwards a small field to the left and then another band of trees. Beyond these trees, turn left onto a rough path.

5 When the path joins a clearer track turn left, leaving the trees to your left.

6 When the track joins a public road, turn left into the little village of Broadmoor, then go on along the clear track beyond.

7 After a short way this track joins a clearer track which comes from the left. Continue along this until it reaches a hairpin bend.

8 Do not follow the bend, but take the rough footpath that continues straight ahead.

9 Turn right at a clear four-way junction. Continue until the path almost reaches the road, then turn left and follow a clear path through the woods, over another junction and back to the car park.

Points of interest

A Leith Hill Tower is an 18th-century folly which stands on the summit of the highest point in south-east England. The stone tower brings the 965 ft (294 m) high hill up to more than 1000 ft (305 m). On a clear day, 13 counties can reputedly be seen from the top of the tower.

B Antsiebury Hill Fort is characteristic of the few Iron Age relics in Surrey. Sandy bastions like this site were important in developing isolated fortified settlements.

C Wotton House was the family home of the 18th-century diarist John Evelyn. Much of the wooded territory in this walk is the product of a planting project he undertook on what was the Evelyn estate.

Walk 12
SHERE AND HACKHURST DOWNS

5 miles (8 km)
Mixed difficulty (mostly easy)

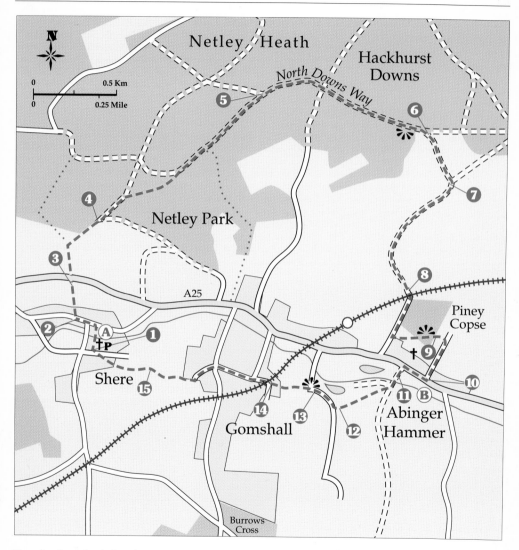

Shere has been lauded as the prettiest village in Surrey. This walk takes in its attractions, and those of two adjacent villages, and covers a pleasant stretch of the North Downs Way across Netley Heath and Hackhurst Downs. There are far-reaching views from several points on the route, across the Vale of Tilling Bourne and of the surrounding downs. To reach the start of the route, come off the M25 at junction 9 (near Leatherhead) and take the A24 south to the edge of Dorking. Then turn right at the roundabout onto the A25 and drive west for 5 miles (8 km) until reaching Shere village. Take the first left turn into the village, then turn left again into the square. There is limited parking space beside the church. PUBLIC TRANSPORT: Take the Portsmouth train from London Waterloo and change at Guildford for Gomshall to start the walk at ⑬ (this is off Wonham Way on the far side of the A25).

Route description

❶ Begin behind the church in the graveyard. Follow the footpath as far as the road, then turn left along the road.

❷ A short way on, turn right at East Lodge and follow the track along the edge of Shere Recreation Ground.

❸ Pass through the tunnel beneath Shere by-pass (A25) and continue straight ahead uphill, then bear right.

❹ At the divide, ignore the right fork and continue along the uphill track, then fork right at the following junction (100 yards beyond the pillbox). Proceed to the top of the hill, then take the left fork.

❺ Turn right at the T-junction and follow the surfaced lane across Netley Heath (North Downs Way) for the next mile (1.6 km). Follow the lane around the 'S' bend and proceed straight ahead at the next major junction.

❻ At the end of a straight section of lane (past the wooden seat and viewpoint on the right), fork right at the yew trees. (The lane forms a loop at this point.) Proceed onto Hackhurst Downs, but fork left after 100 yards (watch for the 'acorn' sign) to continue along the North Downs Way.

❼ Proceed as far as the next junction, then turn right and follow the well-defined track downhill.

❽ At the bottom of the hill walk through the railway tunnel, then proceed towards the woods 100 yards to the left. Continue along the track to the far end of the short stretch of woodland, then turn left and follow the footpath uphill into Piney Copse.

❾ Cross the stile at the end of Piney Copse, proceed along the right-hand edge of the field, cross the next stile and turn right along the lane.

❿ Continue until reaching the main road at Abinger Hammer. Cross over and turn right. Walk beside the main road for a few minutes, past the old watercress beds. Turn left at the '30' sign (before the bus stop) and proceed past the cottages.

⓫ Cross the bridge over the River Tilling Bourne. A few steps on, fork half-left through the small gateway, then continue along the footpath. (Ignore the next gateway, which leads to a private house.)

⓬ On reaching a private road, turn right and proceed to the first bend.

⓭ When the road bears right proceed almost straight ahead and follow the footpath beside the double wooden gates, parallel to the farm track. Pass through the small gate at the far end and continue along the edge of the farmyard to the road.

⓮ Turn right and go through the tunnel, then turn left. Proceed to the next junction and cross straight over it into Gravelpits Lane. After a short distance, turn right where the lane bears left (between 'Highlands' and 'Gravelpits Farmhouse') and continue along the obvious route to the small gate.

⓯ Go through the small gate and follow the right-hand edge of the next field. Before the field ends, pass through the small gate on the right and continue down the footpath towards Shere church. Pass through the final gate to emerge where the walk began.

Points of interest

Ⓐ St James's Church, one of the finest in England, was carefully restored between 1956 and 1966. The site is thought to have accommodated a church since the 7th century—a Saxon church was mentioned in the Domesday Book (1087). The present building dates from the 12th century and much of the original structure still survives. The massive oak door on the south side was built about 1200, and the Purbeck marble font was made in the 13th century. Another interesting feature inside the church is the anchoress's cell in the north wall. In 1329 Christine Carpenter, daughter of the local carpenter, volunteered to be anchoress; she was walled up in the cell leaving only a small hole through which she received food and watched the Mass.

Ⓑ Abinger Hammer is an attractive village, remarkable for its Victorian tilehung houses, striking clock and ponds. The ponds are now used as watercress beds, but their original purpose was to provide the water-power needed to operate the forges and drop-hammers of the medieval iron industry. In 1950 a Mesolithic pit dwelling (at least 5000 years old) was discovered in Abinger parish. It is one of the earliest man-made shelters found in Britian and is possibly the best example of Mesolithic remains in Europe.

Walk 13
WINKWORTH ARBORETUM

2 miles (3 km)   Easy

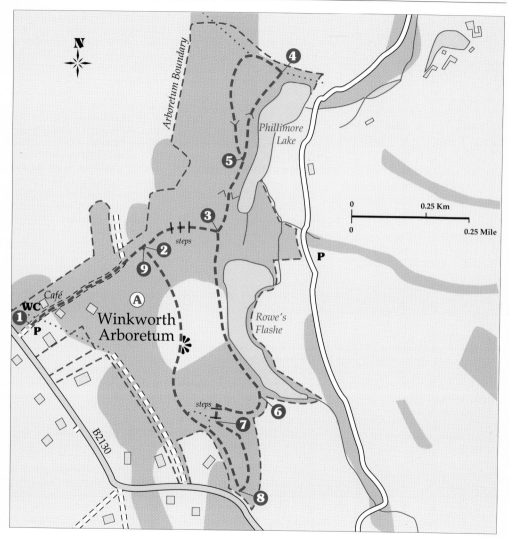

A short route in pleasant mixed woodland, along some of the variety of paths inside the National Trust owned arboretum. To reach Winkworth Arboretum, leave the M25 at junction 10 and drive towards Guildford on the A3. Turn off at the third major roundabout and follow the signs to Godalming along the A3100. From the town centre, take the B2130 south for 2 miles (3.2 km) until reaching the entrance and car park on the left. There is a charge to enter the arboretum (telephone 01483 208477 for details). PUBLIC TRANSPORT: Take the Portsmouth train from London Waterloo to Godalming, then Tillingbourne bus 42 or 44 from Godalming High Street to the arboretum (Mon-Sat only).

Route description

1 Walk out of the back of the car park along the main track, continuing until it splits.

2 At the junction, head left, then down a flight of steps and onward.

3 When the path joins up with the another clear track, turn left and walk along the bottom of the slope beside Phillimore Lake.

4 On reaching the far end of the lake, turn left up a rough path then left again to double back along a track further up the slope (forming a loop).

5 When the path rejoins the lakeside track, continue back towards the start, but ignore the right-hand turn which leads to the car park and proceed straight on beside another lake: Rowe's Flashe.

6 Continue until reaching the edge of the arboretum, then follow the track up the slope to the right and around to the left, up a flight of steps.

7 Turn left at the top of the steps and follow the path through rough, broad-leaved woodland until it almost reaches the road.

8 Stay on the path as it climbs slightly and doubles back, quickly becoming a clearer track which emerges from the woods into open parkland and runs along the top of the slope above the lakes.

9 At the T-junction half a mile (0.8 km) on, turn left to get back to the car park.

Point of interest

A Winkworth Arboretum was originally planted by Dr Wilfred Fox before the Second World War. It is a splendid semi-wild garden laid out across the steep slopes overlooking two small lakes, and it is crossed by numerous footpaths. The arboretum contains many rare trees and shrubs and provides habitat for abundant wildlife. It is arguably most attractive in the spring when there is an impressive display of bluebells and azaleas.

Walk 14
OCKLEY COMMON

2.5 miles (4 km)   Easy

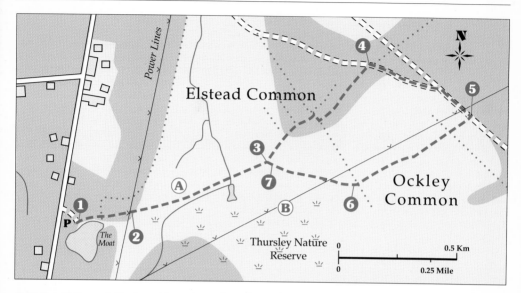

A level walk through fine broad-leaved woods and open heathland that passes beside a nature reserve. To reach the start of the route, leave the M25 at junction 10 and take the A3 as far as Milford—6 miles (9.7 km) beyond Guildford. Turn off at the Milford roundabout and get on the B3001 west to Elstead. At the far end of the village, turn left onto the Churt road. A mile and a half (2.4 km) along, turn up a track to the left, signposted 'The Moat', and park in the small car park within a group of pine trees beside the pond. PUBLIC TRANSPORT: Take the Portsmouth train from London Waterloo to Godalming, then Blue Saloon bus 6 from Godalming High Street to Elstead Cock Hill, which is half a mile (0.8 km) north of ❶ (Telephone Surrey traveline—number on page 11—to check service days and times.)

Route description
❶ Walk away from the road, leaving the large pond to your right.
❷ Emerging from the pine trees, continue straight across the moorland and over a small stream.
❸ Ignore the turn-off with duckboards leading into Thursley Nature Park and continue straight ahead into the trees.
❹ At the four-way junction, turn right and follow a clear track along the edge of the woods, with the heath on the right. Stay on the main track as it swings around to the right in an area of birch woodland.
❺ On reaching a line of pylons, turn right along a path parallel to the pylons. Go straight across the next junction and continue onto the heath.
❻ Follow the path as it swings to the right.
❼ When the path meets the original track, turn left to return to the car park.

Points of interest
Ⓐ Elstead and Ockley Commons are typical of the ancient open heathland in western Surrey. They are covered in heather with patches of bracken and birch trees, and criss-crossed by meandering streams and dry sandy tracks.
Ⓑ Thursley Nature Reserve, within Ockley Common, is an area of boggy lowland. It is primarily notable for the large number of dragonfly species it supports.

Walk 15
BROOKWOOD

Up to 4.5 miles (7 km)   Moderate

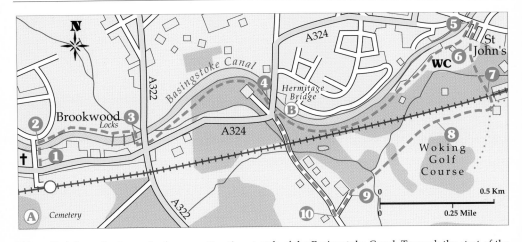

This walk follows the towpath along an attractive stretch of the Basingstoke Canal. To reach the start of the route, leave the M25 at junction 11, taking the A320 into Woking. By-pass the city centre by getting onto the A324 bound for Aldershot. Brookwood is about 3 miles (5 km) west of Woking centre. Park in the town centre, then find the lane that starts directly opposite the entrance to the railway station. PUBLIC TRANSPORT: There are direct trains from London Waterloo to Brookwood.

Route description

1 Walk down to the end of the lane and cross the bridge over the canal.

2 Turn right and follow the towpath past two locks.

3 At the third lock, cross the footbridge over the canal and continue along the far side, under the main road and on through an increasingly rural area of woods and fields.

4 Pass under another road, then continue to a third road bridge at St John's.

From this point, one can either return by the same route or take a slightly longer way back away from the canal, across a golf course and along the road—as described below.

5 Climb up to the road and turn right, then immediately right again.

6 When the road swings around to the right, carry straight on along a tarmac path, heading across an area of open parkland and then into dense woodland.

7 Follow the path across the railway line, then turn right along a path running parallel to the line, with a fence to the right.

8 Turn left up the rough, raised path which leads onto a golf course. Follow the path straight across the course (first making sure that no-one is playing as you cross each hole) and into more woodland.

9 At the end of the path, turn left down a driveway to join the public road.

10 Turn right along the road, keeping a careful watch for traffic. Cross over before reaching the railway bridge, so that you pass under it on the pavement. Then re-cross the road and continue to the junction by Hermitage Bridge. Drop down to the canal and pass under the bridge to backtrack to the start.

Points of interest

A The 2400-acre (970 hectare) landscaped cemetery to the south of Brookwood station was built in 1854 to accommodate an outflow of deceased Londoners, and the railway connection was built especially to transport them. At that time it was the largest graveyard in the world.

B Basingstoke Canal was built by the great canal contractor, John Pinkerton. Completed in 1794, it runs some 40 miles (60 km) from the Wey Navigation to Basingstoke. Initially the canal carried mainly agricultural produce to and from London, then in the 1830s it transported construction materials for the Southern & South Western Railway. Look out for the picturesque houseboats moored by Hermitage Bridge.

Walk 16
WINDSOR FOREST AT BRACKNELL

5.5 miles (9 km)   Easy
except two short, steep sections

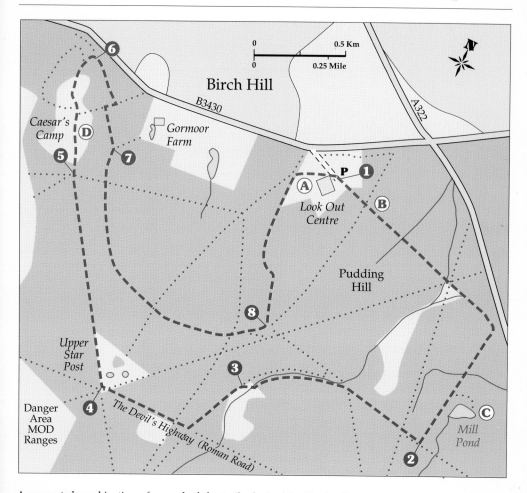

A suggested combination of several of the trails devised by Bracknell Forest Borough Council's leisure department. The forest is a maze of paths, so it is advisable to use an A3 map of the area—available from the heritage centre—alongside this description, and to allow plenty of time in case of wrong turns. To reach the start of the route, leave the M25 at junction 12 and take the M3 south-west to the first junction (junction 3). Take the A322 north through the forest to the roundabout at the edge of the town, then turn left onto the B3430. Half a mile (0.8 km) on, turn left into the entrance to Windsor Forest Look Out heritage centre and take the left fork to the car park. PUBLIC TRANSPORT: Take a train from London Waterloo to Bracknell, then a Bee Line bus to Birch Hill. (The bus station is opposite the railway station. Get off at the stop following Birch Hill shopping centre.)

Route description

❶ From the signpost between the car park and the Look Out heritage centre, walk straight ahead away from the road, on the path signed 'nature trail'. Continue along this broad, straight path, going over the first crossroads and later over a junction with multiple paths. The route draws close to the road, then bends right away from it, up a gentle incline then downhill, past the Mill Pond on the left.

❷ Turn right at the T-junction, slightly uphill. Go straight over the crossroads, where the gradient becomes steeper. At the next junction, fork half-left onto the broad, grassy path and continue along it until the path bends sharply to the right where there is a T-junction.

❸ Turn left and proceed to the next crossroads, then turn right. Almost immediately, go straight over another crossroads and continue to Upper Star Post.

❹ At the post, take the second right fork (signposted 'ladies mile') on the left of the raised clearing (a covered reservoir). Continue ahead, over two crossroads and ignoring several turn-offs.

❺ At the next multiple junction, proceed straight ahead into a clearing signed 'Caesar's Camp'. At the far end of the clearing, continue ahead, ignoring right and left turns. The path leads downhill into thicker forest. Where the main path bends to the left, take the right fork which soon joins a broad sandy path.

❻ Turn right along the sandy path and proceed to the next junction. Bear right at the junction, then turn left almost immediately, initially uphill. The path thins to a very narrow raised path which passes by a clearing on your right, with ramparts beyond. The trees start to close in for a short while, then the path leads steeply uphill.

❼ On emerging onto a clearer path, turn right. Stay on this path for three-quarters of a mile (1.2 km). (The path leads over a four-way junction, inclines slightly uphill, then crosses over another junction and goes downhill through tall pines. It then passes by several turn-offs and goes over another crossroads.) Eventually, bear left at a two-pronged fork.

❽ On reaching a major raised crossroads, turn left (there is a small post with a brown arrow marked 'heritage trail'). Continue, ignoring several turn-offs to the left, until you reach a signposted junction with the heritage centre visible beyond. The car park is just a few yards ahead.

Points of interest

Ⓐ Further information about this area is available from the Look Out heritage centre (telephone 01344 868222). The centre contains a gift shop, café and local history exhibition. Mountain bike hire is available and there is a programme of guided walks and events. Panoramic views may be obtained from the top of a 72 ft (22 m) high tower.

Ⓑ Windsor Forest, which is part of the Crown Estate, contains over 60 species of tree. Scots pines, birches, sweet chestnuts and oaks predominate. Bracken covers the ground, often interspersed with rhododendrons and purple heather along the edges of the paths.

Ⓒ It is well worth diverting at the Mill Pond signpost to take a closer look at this tranquil and delightful pond. Waterlilies float on the water and numerous damselflies and dragonflies hover over it. Look out for them also by the ditches either side of the path and later in the walk where there are smaller ponds off the path at **❹**.

Ⓓ Trees planted in the 1950s are now being cleared from the site of Caesar's Camp, exposing long stretches of ramparts which enclose over 5 acres (13 hectares). The camp is an Iron Age hill fort, probably built around 700 BC by the Atrebatic tribe. The southern entrance used in this route is thought not to be original, but to have been cut to create a 'ride' in the 18th century. There are excellent views of part of the ramparts, featuring a double bank and deep ditches, to the right of the path in the north-east corner of the site. The Look Out centre sells a booklet giving detailed information about Caesar's Camp.

Walk 17
WRAYSBURY LAKES

4 miles (6.5 km) Easy

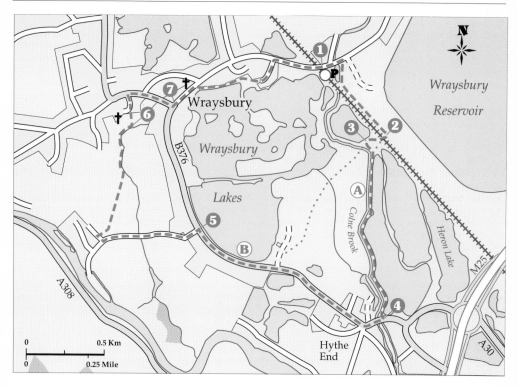

A circuit on clear tracks and pleasant lanes in the southern section of the Colne Valley Park. The majestic lakes and picturesque villages of Wraysbury and Hythe End offer a pleasing contrast to the nearby motorways, airport and dull city suburbs. To reach the start of the route, get on the A30 in west London and where it meets the M25 (junction 13), take the B376 around the west side of the large lake and through Wraysbury to park in the station car park at the far side of the village. PUBLIC TRANSPORT: Direct trains run from London Waterloo to Wraysbury.

Route description

1 Walk out of Wraysbury station's north car park and turn right onto the road. Cross over the road bridge spanning a small stream, then turn right immediately down a small dirt track signposted as a public footpath. The path runs parallel to the stream on your right for 100 yards, then veers away from it to follow the railway line.

2 After 400 yards turn right and cross over the railway line via a wooden stile. Take the path directly in front of you and proceed until you come to a bridge over a small stream in a clearing, but do not cross over the bridge.

3 Turn left and where the path splits into three, take the right-hand fork which runs parallel to the stream for a short distance. At a T-

junction, take the right-hand path that runs between the stream on your right and a large gravel pit on your left.

4 Eventually the footpath meets the road at Hythe End. Cross over a wooden stile and turn right. Walk over the road bridge and continue along the road as it curves around to the right and a large lake later becomes visible on your right.

(There are several places where access to the lakeside is possible.)

5 Turn left down Magna Carta Lane, which is signposted as a public footpath. The lane crosses a small stream. When it splits into two in front of a stone cottage, take the right-hand lane and immediately turn sharp right over a wooden stile into a small field. Follow the path across the field and cross over a small wooden bridge into the next field. Continue over several more stiles and through several small fields, heading towards the church spire in the distance.

6 The footpath eventually reaches the back of St Andrew's Church. Go straight through the grounds of the church to emerge at a small cul-de-sac. Follow the cul-de-sac to the main road and turn right. Proceed past the George Inn and the village green on your left, and over a road bridge to reach a crossroads.

7 Turn left and proceed up to the Baptist church on the left. Take the footpath directly opposite the church, which skirts around the north bank of the large lake. When you get to the road, turn right to return to the start.

Points of interest

Ⓐ Colne Brook is part of a 45-mile (72.5 km) network of river channels (linked to the Thames and the Grand Union Canal) that were historically harnessed to generate power for mills. It is a superb example of an English chalk stream and its crystal clear waters teem with trout and perch which can be seen all year round in the shallow waters at the base of the pools.

Ⓑ Wraysbury Lakes are artificial lakes which were created in the 1960s by flooding gravel pits. They contain a wide diversity of waterfowl, including coots, swans, ducks and herons. Much of the water on the large lake is used by sailing clubs.

Walk 18
HENLEY-ON-THAMES   Up to 5 miles (8 km)   Easy except one climb

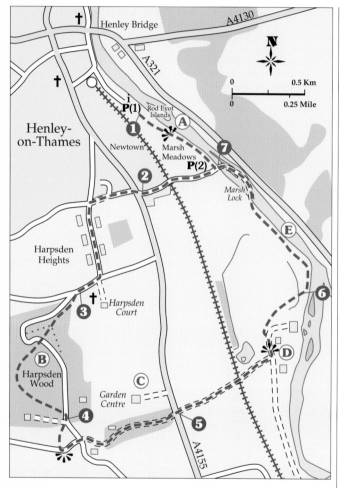

A route covering varied terrain south of Henley, inland along country lanes and through woods, and along a magnificent stretch of the Thames close to the many attractions of Henley town. To reach the start of the route, leave the M25 at junction 15 and take the M4 west to junction 8. Then drive north, past Maidenhead, on the A404 and turn left onto the A4130 to Henley. Having crossed the bridge over the Thames, immediately turn left and continue until the road bends away from the river. Those wishing to cover the entire Thameside section of the route should then turn left into Meadow Road, which ends in a

long car park (1). Alternatively, to avoid seasonal crowds and high parking costs in the centre, continue southward along the main road for half a mile (0.8 km), then turn left along Mill Lane and park in the free car park (2) beyond the bridge over the railway. PUBLIC TRANSPORT: Take the Reading train from London Paddington and change at Twyford for Henley.

Route description
❶ From car park 1, walk down to the river and turn right (away from Henley town). Continue until reaching a lane leading away from the Thames just before the lock horse-bridge. Turn up this lane, passing a car park on your right (car park 2: alternative starting point), and continue over a bridge above the railway and up to the main road.
❷ Bear right and cross the road, then turn left and walk away from the main road along Waterman's Road. When it bends to the right, continue straight on along the footpath to a crossroads. Turn left, cross the road and walk along the pavement on the far side of Harpsden Road. (After a while, the road narrows and the pavement disappears for about 70 yards, so it is necessary to watch carefully for traffic.) Continue around a right bend (walking along the path beside the road) and past Harpsden Court and St Margaret's Church.
❸ Approaching a junction at the portico gateway to the cemetery, look for an unmarked path leading up into woods on the left. Follow the path up a steep slope, keeping parallel to the lane and ignoring turn-offs to the left. On reaching a three-pronged fork, take the middle fork and proceed to the road. Cross

over and continue along the footpath ahead. Keep going (where there is a choice of paths in the woods, take the clearest route each time) until you emerge again onto a lane.

4 Turn right, past a private driveway leading to Red Hatch Lodge, and immediately take a right turn along a narrow fenced footpath leading back into the woods, but which soon meets a lane. Turn left along the lane and proceed to a gateway onto a crossroads, then continue straight on along the stony track. After passing a group of houses, follow the path through a strip of woodland and on to the main road.

5 Cross over and take the path ahead—a broad avenue which leads between fields and past a polo pitch. At the end of the wooden fenced section, go straight ahead uphill and across the bridge over the railway. Continue along the path, now a surfaced 'road', bearing left at the T-junction. Where the road leads into a private driveway, take the footpath on the left which runs parallel to the drive. Pass the big house, then bear left to continue beside the polo pitch.

6 Cross the bridge over the stream and follow the path along the edge of the field, bearing left to walk alongside the Thames. At the far side of the second field, go through the wooden gate and continue along the enclosed path to the lock. Proceed onto the wooden bridge which juts into the Thames and then leads back to the shore further along the bank.

7 At this point, either turn left along the lane back to car park 2, or continue along the riverside, where the path soon opens out onto the green on the left. At the end of the green, cut up to car park 1 on the left.

Points of interest

A The first (and final) stretch of the walk is along the popular Henley waterfront, where smart motorboats are moored and holiday homes cover an island in the river. On the return, fine views of the town may be obtained—including the church tower, seen from a distance over the treetops, and Henley Bridge near the starting point of the Henley Royal Regatta course. From the pier near the start of the walk, hour-long return river trips run upriver along the course to Temple Island and Hambledon (expect long queues on summer weekends).

B These attractive beech and birch woods, where the widely spaced trees allow dappled sunlight to filter onto the path, offer a pleasant deviation from the better-known riverscape in this area.

C Gardening enthusiasts are recommended to turn off the route at **5** and to walk a few yards left along the main road to Engbers Garden Centre. In addition to plants and gardening equipment, there is a pet centre and a coffee shop where walkers can conveniently get a light lunch.

D This small residential outpost contains some of the wealthiest homes in Henley. The footpath leads alongside a magnificent garden containing a large-scale model railway complete with a 2 ft high station!

E On fine weekends, a colourful medley of pleasurecraft (from paddleboats and narrowboats to canoes) share this attractive stretch of the Thames with the swans. More fantastic houses, with manicured gardens down to the river, may be seen on the far bank.

Walk 19
DORNEY AND BOVENEY LOCK

5 miles (8 km)   Easy

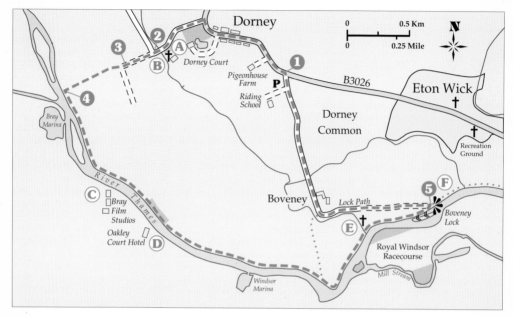

A level, non-strenuous route that is easy to navigate, being mostly along the Thames towpath and quiet lanes, with plenty of places to stop for a picnic. To reach the start of the route, leave the M25 at junction 15 and take the M4 west to junction 6. Then drive south for two-thirds of a mile (1 km) before turning right along Eton Wick Road, through the village and past Dorney Common. Car parking is normally available off the common near the junction with the lane to Boveney (on the left). PUBLIC TRANSPORT: Take the Reading train from London Paddington to Slough and from Slough bus station Bee Line bus 64 towards Maidenhead (Mon-Sat only).

Route description

1 From the eastern edge of Dorney, walk through the village. Pass the gates of Dorney Court on the left, then turn left along a lane and past the church on the left.

2 When the road bends right (Marsh Lane), keep going ahead along a signposted footpath which begins as a track.

3 When the track forks left, keep going ahead (veer slightly right, beside the fence on the right) until reaching the Thames.

4 Turn left at the river and walk alongside it for 2.5 miles (4 km).

5 Pass Boveney Lock on your right, then turn sharp left along the lane back to Dorney Common and the main road.

Points of interest

A Dorney Court is a 15th-century manor house which used to belong to the Abbey of Burnham. It is a beautifully preserved example of Tudor brick and timber framing, and is open to the public afternoons during the Easter weekend, on Sun and Bank hols in May, and Sun-Tue Jun-Sep. The first pineapple to be grown in England was produced here for Charles II.

B The church of St James the Less dates from the 13th century and has a Norman font.

C The Count Dracula horror films were made by Hammer in the now rather delapidated buildings of Bray Studios.

D Oakley Court is now a hotel. It has attractive riverside grounds.

E It is worth diverting to see the chapel of St Mary Magdalene in an isolated spot where there was once a busy wharf. The building dates from the 12th century, but the site is ancient.

F There is a distant view of Windsor Castle on the right.

Walk 20
DENHAM

4.5 miles (7 km)   Easy

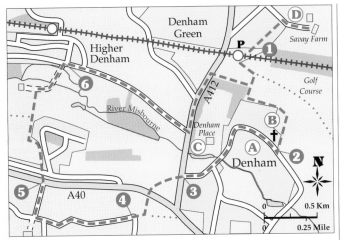

A route that centres on one of the closest truly rural villages to London. To reach the start of the route, take the A40 north-west from central London. Continue on this road across the junction where it meets the beginning of the M40 and soon afterwards turn right along Denham Avenue (A412). Park by St Mary's Church, thereby starting the walk at **2**, or in the station car park (see map for directions). PUBLIC TRANSPORT: Take the High Wycombe train from London Marylebone to Denham. (The walk starts from the south side of platform 1.)

Route description

1 Follow the path away from the station (see above) towards Denham, ignoring a stile on your left and a signposted path on your right. Turn left along a signposted path which follows a fence on your right. Go across a cemetery and turn right towards the church.

2 Turn right along the road towards the centre of the village. Bear left at the tiny green, cross the bridge over the river and bear right to reach the A412.

3 Cross carefully (this is a busy road) to a signposted stile opposite. Go over the stile and veer slightly left across the field to a stile which leads onto a short path. Proceed ahead to the A40, cross via the gap in the hedge in the central reservation and continue ahead on the other side, along an old track. Ignore a signposted path on the left and bear right along the track to a gate.

4 Go through the gate and walk ahead uphill along the lane which enters from the left. Pass Froggy Lane on your left and, opposite Denham Mount, turn right along Mount Lane.

5 Carefully cross the A40 and a subsequent estate road. Proceed ahead along a signposted path between two houses and bear left, as waymarked, to a stile. Cross over the stile and turn right to follow a

fence on your right, down to a stile beside a gate. Continue ahead along a bridleway between hedges. Pass Moorhouse Farm on your left and bear right. Cross the river to reach Higher Denham.

6 Turn right along Lower Road, which leads into Old Rectory Lane. On reaching the A412, cross it carefully and turn left. Turn right through a signposted gap in the hedge and follow the path, which will join up with the outward route. Retrace your steps to Denham station. (To see **D** —Savay Farm— go under the railway, along the footpath to a road, and turn right to the farm.)

Points of interest

A Denham's proximity to film studios led to its charming cottages featuring in several films. The actor Sir John Mills lives in the village.

B St Mary's Church has a 13th-century font and a brass memorial to Agnes Jordan, the last Abbess of Syon at Brentford, who died in 1554. Outside are the graves of seven members of the Marshall family, all murdered on Sunday morning, 22nd May 1870.

C Denham Place was built by Sir Roger Hill between 1688 and 1701. Its grounds were laid out by 'Capability' Brown. In 1729, Sir Roger's son (also Roger) drank himself to death at a 'celebration' after learning of his inheritance in his dying father's will.

D Savay Farm, parts of which date from the 14th century, is the oldest building in Denham. It was once a convalescent home for nuns, who may have bathed in the river. Sir Oswald Mosley lived here before the Second World War and Lady Cynthia Mosley was buried here.

Walk 21
COOKHAM

6 miles (9.5 km)   Easy; muddy parts after rain

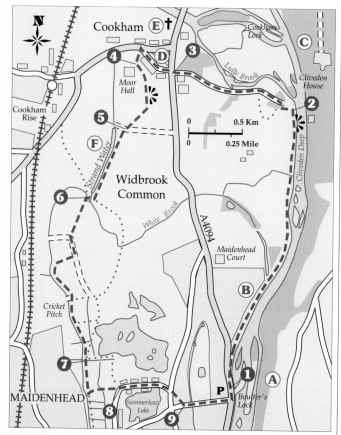

path turns away from the Thames into a copse (this section may be muddy in winter). Continue to the T-junction, then bear right down to the private road. Go left along the road, past a cricket pitch on the right and continue into Cookham village, up to the junction with the main road.

If time permits, it is worth diverting from the route at this point to explore the village (for directions, refer to the map and points of interest Ⓓ and Ⓔ). Rejoin the route via the main shopping street —walk towards the station, then turn left by the war memorial, pass by the left-hand lane and continue from ❹.

❸ To by-pass the village centre, cross the main road, walk a few paces to the right, then turn left along School Lane. At the end, turn left.

❹ Take the narrow footpath on the left, between a thatched cottage and the entrance to Moor Hall (a small sign says 'Green Way East'). Proceed initially between hedges and then between fields, bearing right by a group of conifers.

❺ At the end of the field, cross over the stile and continue straight on along the right-hand edge of another cultivated field, with a stream running parallel on your right. Continue straight on through a second field, then turn right at the junction and cross the bridge over the stream. Follow the narrow path (this short section can get a bit overgrown or muddy), then cross over the concrete bridge.

❻ Turn left and walk along the path through the middle of a field. At the next junction, turn left along a gravel track. After a short distance, turn right into a field

It is well worth traversing a built-up area to complete this interesting route, which incorporates a popular section of the Thames path. To reach the start of the route, leave the M25 at junction 15, driving west along the M4 to junction 8, then get on the A308 and go north. Approaching the centre of Maidenhead, bear right to the Thames, then drive north to Boulter's Lock. Park in the car park opposite the lock. PUBLIC TRANSPORT: Trains run regularly from London Paddington to Maidenhead.

Route description

❶ Cross the road from the car park to Boulter's Lock, turn left and walk along the path by the side of the Thames. (The road initially runs parallel, then bears away from the river leaving a more rural scape.)

❷ 1.5 miles (2.4 km) upriver, the

(signposted 'Green Way West') and proceed along the path to the bottom, then turn left and walk along the bottom of two fields beside the stream, ignoring paths to the left. Continue past a bridge and cricket pitch on the right.

7 At the end of the field cross the bridge ahead, then continue straight on with the stream now on your left. Take the next left turn and follow the path to the road.

8 Bear left, then walk straight ahead along the pavement of the residential street until reaching a junction with a main road. Cross the road and take the footpath to the right of a residential close.

9 On emerging onto a road, turn left. Proceed to the river and turn left to get back to the start of the route.

Points of interest

A Boulter's Lock is one of the busiest locks on the Thames. The number of craft passing through it escalated during the late Victorian and Edwardian periods, when colourful punting parties were held along Cliveden Reach.

B The path along the west bank of the river above Boulter's Lock passes by the fringes of suburban Maidenhead, where gardens of large houses sweep down towards the river, then becomes a pretty tree-lined avenue. Beyond this there are fields on the left and wild flowers at the water's edge. Ducks and pleasure craft claim the river and, on the far side, dense lush woodland predominates until, nearing Cookham, clearings reveal a gabled cottage (with tall gothic chimneys) on the bank and later a circular folly on the hillside.

C Cliveden House stands 200 ft (61 m) above the river amidst the beech woods of its vast estate. (If it cannot be glimpsed above the trees from the Thameside path—just before it turns inland—it is possible to get a more distant view at **4** through a gap in the hedge on the left). Built in 1851 by Charles Barry, the architect of the Houses of Parliament, the Italianate house was the scene of political intrigues by the 'Cliveden Set' in the 1930s and the Profumo affair in the 1960s.

D The Stanley Spencer Gallery, in a former Wesleyan Chapel, contains a selection of his paintings of Cookham, where Spencer lived. It opens Easter-Oct 10.30–17.30 daily, 11.00–17.00 Sat, Sun and Bank hols only in winter.

E Stanley Spencer's famous Last Supper is in the chancel of Cookham Church.

F The Green Way is a series of watercourses fed by the Thames, which were originally created to drain the farmland. It provides a 'corridor' for wildlife that incorporates a variety of habitats from hedgerows to streams and gravel lakes.

Walk 22
MILTON'S COTTAGE

5.5 miles (9 km)   Easy

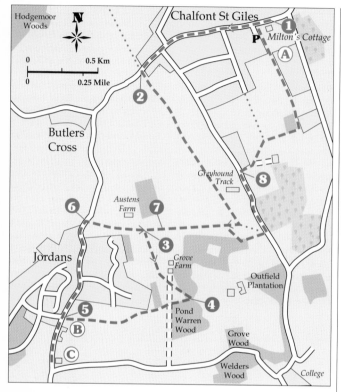

A route through very tranquil countryside, despite the proximity of roads and houses. It is recommended that you go on this walk when the pretty Milton's Cottage is open (see Ⓐ). To reach the start of the route, take the A40 north-west from central London (or leave the M25 at junction 16, driving east to join the A40). Turn onto the A413 before crossing under the M25 and continue along this road until reaching the turn-off for Chalfont St Giles. Drive straight along the High Street, past Milton's Cottage on the left, and park in Hillside Close.
PUBLIC TRANSPORT: Take the High Wycombe train from London Marylebone to Gerrards Cross then, from The Packhorse pub, Chilternrover bus 305 (towards High Wycombe) or 353 (towards Berkhamsted). Infrequent Sunday service on bus 353 only.

Route description

❶ With your back to Milton's Cottage (and facing Milton's Restaurant), turn left to walk up to a roundabout. Go ahead to a public footpath signposted on your left.
❷ Take the well-defined left-hand path. Pass a greyhound training

track on your left, continue past woodland and turn right along a path to a stile ahead, in the left-hand corner of the field. Walk along the right-hand side of the hedge, then go through a kissing gate to the corner of the next field.
❸ Ignore the stile ahead and turn left over another stile. Walk to the left of the hedge, crossing three stiles, and veer left to the far corner of the field. Cross a farm access lane, via the stiles in the fences on either side, and continue but do not go ahead across the stile in the far corner of the field.
❹ Turn sharp right to follow the path with the wood on your left, back to a stile onto the farm access lane. Cross to a stile beside a gate and proceed on the left-hand side of the hedge. Cross over a stile and go ahead, over another stile, to reach the road at Jordans.
❺ Turn left to see the Quaker Guest House, the Mayflower Barn and the Friends Meeting House, then retrace your steps up the road. Continue beyond the entrance to the footpath you have just walked along, and proceed through the village to the next public footpath on your right.
❻ Turn right along the footpath to a gate. Continue along the well-defined path, passing Austens farmhouse on your left. Cross over a stile in the hedge ahead to rejoin your outward path and retrace your steps with the hedge now on your right.
❼ Go ahead through the kissing gate and continue to the corner of the next field, but do not go over the stile ahead. Turn right over another stile and proceed ahead to a field. Veer left to a hedge in the left-hand corner, then turn left along the path

44

between hedges which leads to the road. Cross the road, turn left and walk along the pavement.

8 Turn right along a signposted path and fork left. At the next fork, bear right and proceed to another signposted footpath. Turn left along this path and follow it to the road, passing playing fields on your left. At the road, turn right to get back to Milton's Cottage.

Points of interest

A This small cottage is the only one of John Milton's homes still standing. It was found for the poet by his former pupil, Thomas Ellwood. Milton fled to Chalfont St Giles from London to avoid the plague and lived there for just one year, from May 1665 to April 1666, during which time he completed the epic poem *Paradise Lost*—dictated by the then blind Milton to his daughter Deborah.

Ellwood was unable to welcome Milton to his new abode because he had been arrested at the funeral of fellow Quaker, Edward Perot. (Perot had tried to convert the pope in order to end the persecution of Presbyterians under Charles II.)

Upon his release, Ellwood visited Milton at the cottage and was shown a manuscript. After reading it, Ellwood commented, 'Thou hast said much here of paradise lost, but what hast thou to say of paradise found?', clearly referring to his new place of residence. Some time later, when Ellwood was visiting Milton in London, he was presented with *Paradise Regained*.

Milton's Cottage was bought for the nation by public subscription in 1887, in honour of Queen Victoria's Silver Jublilee (with the Queen herself donating £20). It is now open to the public Mar-Oct, daily except Mon. Opening hours are 10.00-13.00 and 14.00-18.00 Tue-Sat and on Spring and Summer Bank hols; 14.00-18.00 only on Sun.

B Jordans Conference Centre (the Friends Guest House) is a place of pilgrimage for Quakers worldwide, who now own the whole village. Before the Toleration Act of 1688, members of the sect used to meet at the Guest House in secret. The Mayflower Barn is of particular interest because it is built from timbers taken from the *Mayflower*—the ship that took the Pilgrim Fathers to America. Salt has impregnated the wood and one of the beams, thought to be from the ship's stern, bears the letters R HAR I—all that remains of MAYFLOWER HARWICH. The barn is still used in the summer for concerts and other events.

C The Meeting House is a simple structure built in 1688 following the passing of the Toleration Act. Lady Springett, the widow of leading Quaker Isaac Pennington, provided the funds. Outside are the graves of many early Quakers, including Thomas Ellwood. The preacher William Penn, his two wives, Gulielma and Hannah, and 10 of his 16 children are all buried here. Penn had been arrested for preaching and gathering arms with intent to disturb the peace. The Lord Mayor of London famously fined and jailed his jurors for twice finding Penn not guilty of the latter charge. This was appealed against and found to be unlawful, thus striking a blow against the suppression of freedom of speech. Penn later emigrated to America, where he founded the State of Pennsylvania on Quaker principles.

Walk 23
HUGHENDEN MANOR

3 miles (5 km)   Moderate

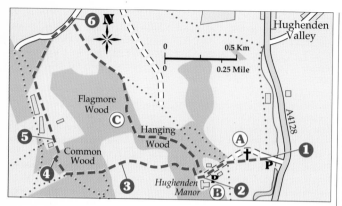

A route that encapsulates the essence of Buckinghamshire: a magnificent country setting containing a manor house that belonged to a famous politician. To reach the start of the route, leave the M25 at junction 16 and drive west on the M40 to High Wycombe. Exit the motorway at junction 4 and take the A4128 north. Two miles (3.2 km) on, turn left into a lane signposted to Hughenden Manor. Park in the lay-by just before reaching the church or, if visiting the manor, in the private car park further along. PUBLIC TRANSPORT: Take a train from London Marylebone to High Wycombe, then Chilternrover bus 323 or 324 from Newlands bus station to the manor lane entrance (by the Hughenden Manor signpost). There is an infrequent Sunday service on bus 325.

Route description

1 Start the walk in the churchyard, passing to the left of the church. Go ahead along the uphill path to a small gate, which leads to a lane. Bear left along the lane, passing Hughenden Manor on your left.

2 Go down a signposted bridleway through the trees. Ignore paths on either side and continue until emerging from the woodland onto a fenced path.

3 Proceed ahead to enter more woods. Keep to the main path ahead, ignoring other paths. Pass a small gate on your right and turn right along a clear track just beyond it.

4 Fork right to follow a bank of earth on your right. Cross over a stile ahead and walk between a house on your left and a field on your right, to a kissing gate.

5 Go ahead along a track. After the last house on your left, cross over a stile ahead and bear right through the wood, with its edge never far away on your right. On reaching a lane at a signpost, turn right.

6 A short way along the lane, turn right over a stile to follow a signposted path. Cross over the stile in the corner of the field, then walk beside the hedge on your right until reaching woodland on

the right. Look out for a stile in the fence and go over it to bear left along a woodland path. Bear right along a forest track and stay on this path all the way back to Hughenden Manor. Then retrace your steps back to the start.

Points of interest

A The Church of St Michael and All Angels is where Disraeli (Prime Minister 1868 and 1874-80) chose to be buried. He was perhaps the greatest statesman of many politicians born in Buckinghamshire. Queen Victoria, who regarded 'Dizzy' with much affection, visited the church soon after his burial in 1881 and laid a wreath of Disraeli's favourite primroses on his tomb. Disraeli's admirers wore primroses in their buttonholes on the first anniversary of his death on 19th April, thereby starting the Primrose League.

B Hughenden Manor was bought by Disraeli in 1847 and he lived there until his death. Now owned by the National Trust, the house contains much of Disraeli's furniture as well as personal possessions. The primroses that Queen Victoria brought to his grave are also displayed. Hughenden Manor opens to the public during March 13.00–17.00 at weekends only, and Apr-Oct Wed-Sun and Bank hol Mon 13.00–17.00 (except Good Friday).

C The Hanging and Flagmore Woods formed part of the Hughenden Manor Estate and are shaped by Disraeli's tree planting schemes. They are most beautiful in the spring, when bluebells flower under the beech trees, and in autumn.

Walk 24
GREAT MISSENDEN   4 miles (6 km)   Moderate; can be muddy in places

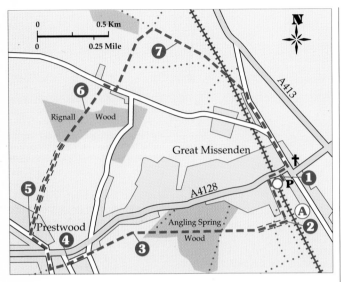

An easily accessible route through some great walking country with clearly waymarked paths in generally good condition (except for mud in wet weather), and featuring attractive woods with bluebells in May. To reach the start of the route, leave the M25 at junction 18 and take the A404 west to Amersham. From there get onto the A413 north to the Great Missenden turn-off. Go into town on the A4128 and park in the station car park. PUBLIC TRANSPORT: Take the Aylesbury train from London Marylebone to Great Missenden.

Route description

1 Turn left out of the station car park and left again to cross the bridge over the railway. Turn left down a private road (which is a public path) and continue past Bernards Close on your right.

2 Turn right up a track, passing a cemetery on your left, and proceed ahead into woods. Ignore a signpost on your right in the woods and continue ahead through a kissing gate to walk on the left-hand side of a hedge.

3 Go ahead across a field to pick up the hedge on your right again and continue along a narrow path between houses to a road. Go ahead along the New Road opposite.

4 Cross another road and continue along the narrow hedged footpath facing you. Turn right at another road (Nairdwood Lane), then cross the main road to go up Moat Lane.

5 Turn right up the concrete driveway to Prestwood Farm. Follow the sign to a stile ahead. Go over a second stile and then a third, ignoring tracks on either side.

Proceed ahead with the hedge on your right. The path converges with a track on your right, then forks right into the woods. Continue through the trees, ignoring turn-offs on the right.

6 Leave the woods by the narrow path ahead, with a fence on your right and a hedge on your left. Go down to the road and turn right along it. Turn left up a signposted path and veer left as waymarked 'GM70'. Bear right through trees to the ridge, then turn right to walk on the left-hand side of the hedge, down to the gap in the bottom corner of the field.

7 Follow the path straight ahead across the next field and over a waymarked stile on the right. Proceed to a tunnel under the railway on your left, go through the tunnel and cross a stile in the corner of the field. Turn right along the road and right again, as signposted, to the station.

Point of interest

A There was once an abbey on this site, which was on a major route to London. It was built out of gratitude by William de Missenden in 1133, after he was rescued from a shipwreck. The abbey's position ensured that it soon became large and wealthy, and it received many donations. The resident monks, known as the Black Canons, wielded great influence locally, but spiritual corruption followed and an Abbot was dismissed after a 'visitation' in 1236. Another Abbot had a scandalous relationship with a woman in 1530—shortly before Henry VIII's dissolution of the monasteries.

Walk 25
TRING RESERVOIRS

2 miles (3 km)   Easy

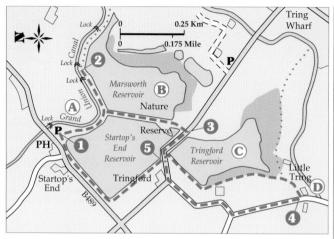

Points of interest

Ⓐ The Grand Union Canal links the Thames in London with Birmingham, Leicester and Nottingham. It was intended to be an important means of commercial transport, but was soon superseded by the railway. The construction of this section of the canal set new standards for wide locks. A rise of nearly 40 ft (120 m) made it necessary to build many locks, including the six locks known as 'Tring steps'. Four reservoirs were dug to supply water through the locks to maintain the canal's upper level. Fed by natural springs, the reservoirs are marl lakes, found only in chalk and limestone areas. They were designated a National Nature Reserve in 1955, as the minerals in the water support an abundance of plants and fish.

Ⓑ Marsworth Reservoir is renowned for its wildfowl. A few of the many types of bird often seen on the lake are: lots of duck species, including tufted ducks (with black crests and white flanks), pochards (with chestnut coloured heads) and gooseanders (fish-eating ducks with a bottle-green head and rosy-pink body); coots, dabchicks and bitterns (in winter); and great crested grebes. The latter, whose courtship displays can be seen between December and May, were studied here by biologist Julian Huxley. Herons nest in the trees beside the reservoir and the reed beds contain a large colony of reed warblers, which return annually from their migration to Africa.

Ⓒ Tringford Reservoir has particularly rich vegetation on its bank. You may see woodpeckers in the trees. Migrant wading birds, such as green and common sandpipers, can be seen from the hide.

Ⓓ The pumping station, which controls the flow of water into the canal, is on your left.

A short walk for naturalists, which will be particularly interesting for bird-watchers. To reach the start of the route, leave the M25 at junction 20 and drive north-west on the A41. Continue straight over the Tring roundabout and just over a mile further on turn right along the B489. Drive past Wilstone Reservoir and keep going until just past the second reservoir in Startop End, where there is a car park on the right (before reaching the bridge over the canal). PUBLIC TRANSPORT: Take the Northampton train from London Euston to Tring, then bus 27 or T3 (Mon-Sat) from the station to New Mill Estate, which is just off the map in the top right-hand corner (go straight over the crossroads and continue for half a mile (0.8 km) to start the walk at ❸).On Sun take Chiltern Ramblers' bus 327 to Tringford and start at ❺ (infrequent service, summer only).

Route description

❶ From the back of the car park, go to the edge of the reservoir and turn left. Walk along the left-hand edge of the reservoir with the Grand Union Canal down on your left. Proceed past a right turn between reservoirs, to a lock.

❷ Retrace your steps from the lock to the turn-off now on your left. Walk between the reservoirs to a road ahead.

❸ Turn right along the road until reaching a stile on the left. Go over the stile and follow a narrow path through woodland, with the reservoir on your left. Pass a hide on your left and continue to a stile beside a gate on the right. Cross over the stile onto a lane and walk ahead to a junction.

❹ Turn right along the road and bear right at a fork. Bear right again at another fork and continue until you see a signposted footpath on your left.

❺ Go through the gap in the hedge on the left and follow the path around the left-hand edge of the reservoir. Keep going until you get back to the car park.

Walk 26
TELEGRAPH HILL

4 miles (6 km)   Moderate

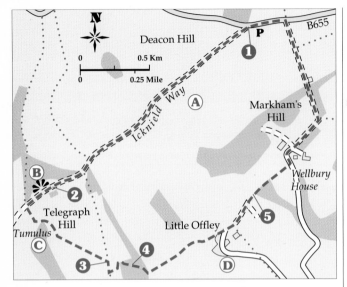

field. Go ahead with a hedge on your right. Pass the Tudor house at Little Offley on your right and continue ahead along a bridleway. When the farm track bends to the right, keep going straight down a field path.

5 Pass a patch of woodland on your right and proceed ahead across the corner of the field. Turn left along an access lane to pass Wellbury House on your right, then go ahead along a rough track on the right-hand edge of a field. Bear left to pass by a junction on your right. Pass a cottage called 'Woodland' on your right and go ahead along a track to the B655. Turn left and walk carefully along the road back to the start.

Points of interest

A The Icknield Way is an ancient route along the chalk 'spine' of southern England. It links with the Ridgeway at Goring to provide a through route from Norfolk to Dorset (now mainly along roads) and runs parallel to the higher Ridgeway into Wiltshire. The section featured in this walk is one of the best preserved. The county boundary between Hertfordshire and Bedfordshire runs down the centre of the track and excellent views may be obtained over Bedfordshire on the right.

B Telegraph Hill was the site of a semaphore signalling station used by the Admiralty to transmit the news of Trafalgar and Waterloo. There used to be a racecourse here and the deep ruts were made by the carriages of race-goers.

C This tumulus (burial mound) is one of many near the Icknield Way.

D King Offa is said to have died near Little Offley.

A short walk along part of the ancient Icknield Way to the beech and birch clothed slopes of Telegraph Hill—thought to have been the object of John Bunyan's eulogy about 'delectable mountains'. To reach the start of the route, leave the M25 at junction 23 and take the A1 north to junction 8, then the A602 to Hitchin. Stay on this road into the town and cross straight over the first roundabout, then turn left at the next major junction, along the B655. Three miles (4.8 km) out of Hitchin, park the car in the lay-by on the left, near the Bedfordshire road sign and the entrance to a bridleway. PUBLIC TRANSPORT: Take a train from King's Cross St Pancras to Luton, then the infrequent Luton & Dunstable bus 79 (Mon-Sat) from the adjacent bus station to Pegsdon (which is a third of a mile or 0.5 km east of **1** along the B655).

Route description

1 Go up the signposted bridle-way, past a stile on your right. The track then climbs gradually for 1 mile (1.6 km) to a waymark post. Pass to the left of the post and, ignoring the signposted bridleway on your left, proceed ahead with the hedge on your right.

2 Pass a group of trees on your left (Telegraph Hill Nature Reserve is beyond them). Go downhill to a junction and turn left. Climb up the path to pass a tumulus on your right, then bear left across a field.

3 Pass a signpost and proceed, with the hedge on your right, to another sign. Turn left here, across a field to the corner of a wood. Walk to the left of the trees for 20 yards, then bear right along a path into the wood.

4 The path curves left through the wood to emerge in the corner of a

Walk 27
VERULAMIUM

7.5 miles (12 km)   Easy

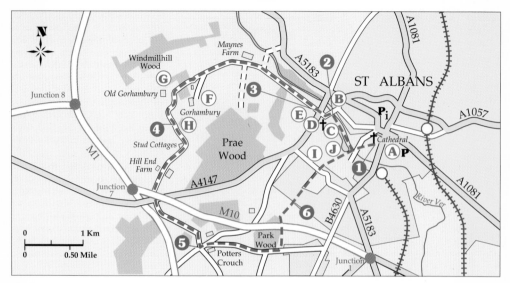

The main attractions of this walk are the remnants of the Roman city, and the awe-inspiring cathedral. The route is easy to follow, but walkers are advised to allow a whole day in order to visit all the places along the way. Note that the private road between ❸ and ❺ is closed on 1st May every year. To reach the start of the route, leave the M25 at junction 21 and take the A414 up to where it joins the M10, then turn off onto the A5183 and follow the signs to the cathedral. There are several signposted car parks nearby. PUBLIC TRANSPORT: Trains run regularly from King's Cross Thameslink station to St Albans.

Route description

❶ Start from the Chapter House and Visitor Centre on the south side of the cathedral. With the Chapter House behind you, turn half-right to follow a footpath running diagonally towards the River Ver. Pass Ye Olde Fighting Cocks pub on your right, cross the bridge on your left and turn right to follow a path between the lake (on the left) and the River Ver (on the right).

❷ On reaching St Michael's Street, turn left (see Ⓑ, Ⓒ and Ⓓ). Continue to the A4147 and cross the pelican crossing to the private road opposite.

❸ Go ahead along the estate lane, passing the Roman theatre on your left. Ignore the waymarked 'Ver Walk' on your right and continue past Maynes Farm. When the lane forks just before Gorhambury, go right to pass the house on your left. Bear left with the lane, then right, passing the ruins of Old Gorhambury on your right.

❹ Pass Temple Cottages on your left and proceed downhill. Follow the lane around to the right to pass Stud Cottages, and go up the rough track (which becomes a concrete track) to Hill End Farm. Continue under the M10, then carefully cross the A4147 to go ahead along Appspond Lane, with the M1 on your right.

❺ Turn left at Potters Crouch crossroads and fork right at The Holly Bush. Continue past the forest on your left (ignoring the right turn). Then turn left along a signposted footpath, with the forest still on your left, up to the stile ahead. Cross the footbridge over the M10, then cross another stile and follow the path around the trees on your left before turning right to cross a field back towards St Albans.

❻ Follow the path across a grassy area on your left, then bear right up a narrow path between houses. Maintain this direction, crossing three estate roads. Pass a cricket pitch on your right, go ahead across a road at a pelican crossing and follow the footpath ahead beside the

Roman wall. Pass the lake on your left and retrace your steps from Ye Olde Fighting Cocks.

Points of interest

Ⓐ The cathedral and abbey church of St Alban was built on the spot where Alban, England's first Christian martyr, was executed in 209, during the days of the Roman Empire. Offa, king of the Mercians, founded the abbey in 793, which was built from the ruins of the Roman city of Verulamium. The present building was begun by the Normans in 1077. The abbey was dissolved in 1539, but the building was bought by the local people to serve as their parish church. Restored by Lord Grimthorpe in the mid 19th century, it became a cathedral in 1877—the second largest in Britain.

Ⓑ Kingsbury Water Mill is a fully restored and working 16th-century mill. It occupies the site of a mill mentioned in the Domesday Book and is open Tue-Sat 11.00–18.00 and Sun from 12.00 (closes at 17.00 in winter).

Ⓒ Verulamium Museum is open 10.00–17.30 Mon-Sat (and from 14.00 Sun). It contains a large number of finds from the Roman town, including the famous sea god mosaic.

Ⓓ St Michael's Church covers the Roman basilica (town hall) and forum (market place). It has Saxon flint walls incorporating Roman tiles and contains an effigy of Sir Francis Bacon.

Ⓔ This is the only visible Roman theatre in Britain.

Ⓕ Gorhambury was built in the late 18th century. It contains paintings of the Bacon family and is open to the public May-Sep on Thur afternoons (14.00–17.00).

Ⓖ Old Gorhambury, now a ruin, was the family home of Sir Francis Bacon. Some scholars believe he was the true author of some of Shakespeare's plays.

Ⓗ Temple Cottages were built in the mid 18th century as a Palladian-style garden temple.

Ⓘ Verulamium's Roman wall was built about AD200.

Ⓙ The south-east gate (or London gate) was where Watling Street entered the city from the south.

Walk 28
KNEBWORTH PARK

4.5 miles (7 km)   Easy

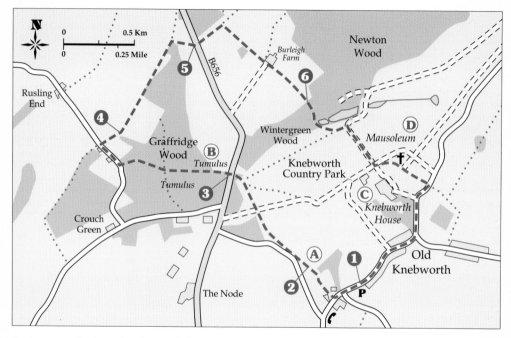

A pleasant walk through a deer park, leading to a country house full of interest and history. To reach the start of the route, leave the M25 at junction 23 and drive north on the A1(M). Exit the motorway at junction 6, just beyond Welwyn Garden City, and take the B656 north to Codicote. Turn right along a minor road to Old Knebworth and park carefully near the Lytton Arms. PUBLIC TRANSPORT: Take a train from London King's Cross to Stevenage, then bus 44 to Old Knebworth (infrequent service, Mon-Sat only).

Route description

1 With your back to the Lytton Arms, cross the road to the pavement and turn left, passing almshouses on your left. Pass the park gatehouse on your right, then turn right over a stile beside a gate. Proceed ahead with a hedge on your right. At the far corner of the field, bear right through woodland and turn left after crossing a stile to go over a ladder stile into the deer park.

2 Pass a monument on your right and keep the hedge on your left.

Follow the path to the right, alongside trees on your left and cross over the ladder stile in the fence ahead. Continue with a fence on your left until you reach another ladder stile. Go over it to get to the road.

3 Cross the road and take the signposted path ahead, over a footbridge and into Graffridge Wood. The path initially keeps to the edge of the wood, then bears left through the trees. Go ahead and continue over a junction and onward to a lane. Turn right, passing Keeper's

Cottage on your left. Just after the second cottage on your left, turn right along a signposted footpath.

4 At the end of the field, go through the gap in the hedge and continue alongside the right-hand edge of the next field, then pass a wood on your right. Go ahead over a stile beside a gate and cut across the field to wooden bars in the fence on the right of the opposite corner. Go ahead through scrub, then bear right to a stile in the corner of the field and cross over it to climb up to the road.

continued

5 Cross the road and take the signposted path ahead, with woodland on your left. Turn right at a waymark post and follow the path across the field and over a stile beside a gate. Pass a small wood on your right and continue ahead to a farm. Go through the farmyard as signposted and cross a field to a stile beside a gate, then continue straight on across the next field.

6 Take the path ahead into the woodland of Knebworth Park. Veer right at a 'private' sign to follow the public path to a ladder stile in the fence, then turn left along the right-hand side of the fence to a tree-lined concrete track. Turn right along the track to Knebworth House, then bear left to the church. From the back of the churchyard, go through the lych gate and proceed ahead, past the cricket pavilion on your left. Turn right along the road, back to the Lytton Arms.

Points of interest

A This obelisk was erected by Sir Edward Bulwer Lytton in 1866 as a memorial to his mother. He waited until she had been dead 23 years because they had fallen out over his marriage to an unsuitable Irish woman. His mother stopped his allowance and his late father's bequest could not support his new wife's extravagant lifestyle. The marriage subsequently failed due to lack of money, although Edward Bulwer later became a successful novelist and Member of Parliament. Bulwer anticipated Dickens in his early novels, which criticised the harsh penal code and appalling prison conditions of his time. Mystic romanticism crept into his later novels, such as *The Last Days of Pompeii,* and in *The Coming Race* he prophesied the destructive force of nuclear weapons. Bulwer and Dickens together founded the Guild of Literature and Art and put on dramatic performances in Knebworth's banqueting hall to subsidise poor 'men of letters'. As a Liberal politician, Bulwer campaigned for the victims of 'low birth and iron fortune'. However, friendship with Disraeli led him to cross the floor of the House. One of his speeches as Colonial Secretary was described by Palmerstone as the best he had ever heard in the House of Commons.

B Look for a Bronze Age tumulus to the right of the path as it enters Graffridge Wood.

C The original Knebworth was a small manor house owned by a knight called Eudo Dapifer, a steward to William the Conqueror. It is recorded in the Domesday Book as Chenepeworde, meaning 'the house on the hill'. The Lytton family came here in 1492 (the first Earl of Lytton, who was also first Viceroy of India, lived at Knebworth) and it remained an essentially Tudor building until the 19th century, when Edward Bulwer Lytton modernised it in Victorian Gothic style. The towers were capped with copper domes and the house was embellished with battlements and gargoyles, although the east front retains a Tudor appearance and the banqueting hall where Elizabeth I was entertained has a minstrels' gallery dating from 1610 and a Jacobean oak screen. Knebworth House and gardens open Apr-Sep 12.00–17.00 daily. Additional attractions include a collection of railway memorabilia, a model railway and a narrow gauge railway in the park.

D The mausoleum was built in the Grecian style in 1817 to house the remains of Elizabeth Bulwer Lytton. A quarrelsome character, she fell out with the local rector and refused to set foot in the church. The ashes of Lady Constance Lytton, a Suffragette leader, were also set here when she died in 1923.

Walk 29
HERTFORD

3 miles (5 km)   Easy

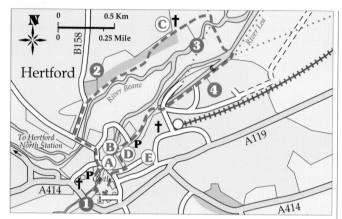

Hertford is a friendly county town, standing where three rivers meet. This walk allows you to explore the castle and enjoy the 'green fingers' of the river valleys that extend into Hertford. To reach the start of the route, leave the M25 at junction 25 and take the A10 north for 9 miles (14.5 km), then the A414 into the centre of Hertford. Park in the Andrew Street car park near the castle. PUBLIC TRANSPORT: Take a train either from London Moorgate (King's Cross Sat and Sun) to Hertford North (half a mile or 0.8 km from **①**), or from London Liverpool Street to Hertford East.

Route description

① From the entrance to the Tourist Information Office in Hertford Castle, turn left past the commemorative stone. Bear right to walk beside the River Lea on your left, then go over two footbridges on your left and bear right over a weir. Turn left over Mill Bridge to Old Cross. (To see **Ⓑ**, turn right down a lane to the right of the library, then return to Old Cross.) Bear right up to Cowbridge and cross the road

bridge over the River Beane, then take the second road on your right (Port Hill). Pass The Reindeer pub on your left before turning right into Warren Meadows.

② Follow the path above the River Beane, which is on your right. Go through St Leonard's churchyard. Leave it on your left and turn right.

③ Take the gravel track around the churchyard on your right and turn left through a kissing gate. Go down the path to cross a footbridge

over the river on your right, then veer left to another bridge, this time over the River Lea. Go across and turn right past Hertford Lock.

④ Follow the towpath to a weir where you switch sides. Pass The Old Barge pub and turn left over Folly Bridge. Go up Bull Plain and turn left into Railway Street (to see **Ⓔ**), then double back to the junction and go ahead up Maidenhead Street. Use the pelican crossing to reach the gates of Hertford Castle ahead.

Points of interest

Ⓐ Hertford Castle was the home of Saxon kings and the venue for the first Christian Synod in England in 673. Notice the Norman motte and bailey and the 12th-century curtain wall.

Ⓑ This is the site of the ford after which Hertford was named.

Ⓒ St Leonard's Church is the oldest surviving church in Hertford. It has a Saxon font, a leper squint and the remains of an anchorite's cell.

Ⓓ Hertford Museum (on your left) is open Tue-Sat 10.00-17.00. Admission is free.

Ⓔ Number 13 Railway Street was once the home of Frederick Davis and his wife, who were disturbed at 3.30 am in March 1889 by a man who knocked on their door and asked for an axe to behead his wife. The police were alerted but did nothing for nearly three hours, by which time it was too late.

Walk 30
WIDFORD

5.5 miles (9 km)   Easy

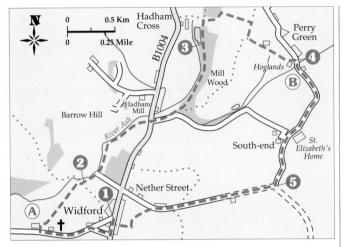

A route through some of the most beautiful countryside in Hertfordshire, in the Ash Valley near the Essex border. To reach the start of the route, leave the M25 at junction 25 and take the A10 north for 7 miles (11.3 km), then turn right along the A414 to Stanstead Abbots and from there take the B180 north to Widford. Park near The Green Man pub. PUBLIC TRANSPORT: Take the Hertford East train from London Liverpool Street to St Margarets, and from there Lea Valley bus 351 to The Green Man (Mon-Sat only).

Route description

❶ From The Green Man pub, walk southward down the main road. Turn right along Bell Lane and at the junction with Abbott's Lane, bear left and walk ahead to the church on your right. Turn right along a path through the churchyard left of the church. Cross over a stile and descend the rough steps, then follow the well-worn path to a crossing over the River Ash on your left. Continue to a footbridge on your left in the far corner of the meadow, but do not cross it.

❷ Go ahead over a stile and follow the path with the fence on your right. Cross over the lane ahead and proceed along the concrete track to the gates of a waterworks. Turn left along a fenced path which then bears right. Cross the B1004 and go up Bourne Lane. Turn left along a signposted bridleway by the traffic barriers on your left. Ignore a track leading uphill ahead and take the lower left-hand track, which leads past Mill Wood on your right.

❸ Pass a lake on your left, partially hidden by trees, and continue beside a field on your right. At the

junction, turn right over a stile to go uphill with a fence on your left. Skirt around the woods on your left, then turn right along a clear path across the field to a junction by an oak tree. Turn right and proceed to another oak tree, then turn left, passing a farm on your left. At the bottom of the field, bear left over a stile beside a gate to follow a track past the Henry Moore Foundation on your right.

❹ On reaching the lane, turn right along it. Continue for three-quarters of a mile (1.2 km), following the right bend of the road. Pass St Elizabeth's School and Home on your left and at the next bend fork left along a 'no through' road.

❺ At the end of the road, bear right along a gravel track with a hedge on your right and pass a thatched cottage on your left. After the track becomes a lane, turn left over the second signposted stile. Cross over another stile ahead. Turn right through a farmyard to the road, then right along the road back to The Green Man.

Points of interest

Ⓐ St John the Baptist's Church contains some interesting murals dating back to the 13th century. In the graveyard is the grave of Mary Field, grandmother of Charles Lamb, who died in 1792. She was a housekeeper near Widford and was often visited by the young essayist, who wrote endearingly of the village.

Ⓑ Sculptor Henry Moore moved to 'Hoglands' in Perry Green after his studio in London was damaged in 1941. The Henry Moore Foundation is now in his home.

Walk 31
EPPING FOREST

4.5 miles (7 km)   Moderate

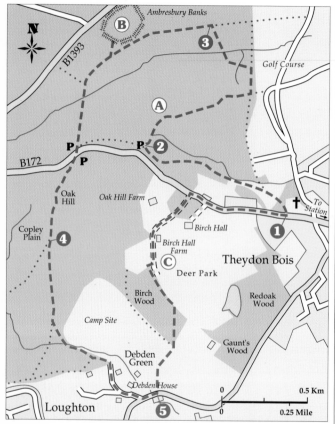

reaching a car park on the left and a crossroads.

❷ Turn right (from the top left exit from the car park, walk directly away from the road) and proceed to a major crossroads. Turn left, then left again onto a narrower path a short way along (just before the golf course comes up to the path on the right). Follow the path along its uneven course through bracken, bearing right where a stream runs on your left (often dried up), then ahead across the bridge over the stream.

❸ Having emerged onto a broad sandy path, turn left and stay on this path, whose surface turns to wood chippings, past **Ⓑ** (divert to the right to see the banks) and beyond a turning to the right. Continue to another car park and walk straight through it to the road. Cross over and proceed ahead along the right-hand edge of the car park on the other side, then continue along the path.

❹ At a two-pronged fork, take the left-hand path ahead which presently goes steeply downhill. As the ground rises again, turn off down to the left, passing a camp site on your left. Proceed across a bridge over a stream and bear left, continuing along the path past a barrier (ignore the path on your right) and onto a surfaced road with houses on either side. Proceed ahead, ignoring a right fork, to the main road.

❺ Cross over, turn left and walk along the pavement to the corner. Then turn left along a signposted bridleway, up the hill past a turn-off on the left and into the trees where the gradient levels. Continue on the winding path through the woods.

The continued conservation of Epping Forest as a large, unshrinking rural area on the very edge of London is astonishing. This route takes in some of the northern forest where the city seems 100 miles away. To reach the start of the route, get on the M11 in north-east London. Leave the motorway just beyond Chigwell and take the A1168 through Loughton. At the junction with the A121, turn right up Golding's Hill. Take the B172 from the roundabout and proceed to the car park on the left (start from stage **❷**). PUBLIC TRANSPORT: Take the Underground central line (Epping branch) to Theydon Bois.

Route description

❶ Fifty yards west of St Mary's Church (on the main road), turn right at an Epping Forest sign where

there is a small park ahead. Turn left along the footpath leading into the trees and continue along the main path, ignoring turn-offs, until

56

At the far end, walk up to a track on the right and continue ahead. The track eventually becomes a surfaced driveway and soon afterwards meets the main road. Turn right to go back to Theydon Bois or left to return to the car park.

Points of interest

(A) A former Royal Forest and hunting ground, Epping Forest has been managed by the Corporation of London since 1878, and since that time its size has increased significantly to over 6300 acres (2500 hectares). The woodland is ancient (there is evidence that it began to develop after the Ice Age) and commoners have had grazing rights on the land since Anglo-Saxon times, when the practice of coppicing the oaks, beeches and hornbeams to obtain firewood also begun.

Look out for the characteristic multiple trunks of coppiced trees and the gnarled effect caused by pollarding. Young trees were cut a couple of metres above ground (or above head height in pollarding so that deer and cattle would not eat the new shoots) on a 15–20 year cycle. Wildlife has benefited from the resultant variation between different areas of forest, 70% of which is now a Site of Special Scientific Interest. In particular, there are over 1000 species of fungi (seen on decomposing trunks) and many species of rare wood-boring beetles. The forest's conservators are now reviving or simulating traditional practices to maintain the ancient habitats. Pollarding has been restarted, mowing compensates for declining numbers of grazing animals, and scrub and birch trees are being cleared to restore rare heathland (for example, at Long Running south-west of Ambresbury Banks). There is an Epping Forest Conservation and Information Centre at High Beach near Loughton.

(B) Ambresbury Banks is one of two Iron Age hill forts within the forest. According to legend, it was the base from which Boadicea set out to fight her last battle with the Romans.

(C) Black fallow deer—unique to Epping Forest—are now preserved in a 100-acre (40 hectare) enclosure.

Walk 32
HATFIELD FOREST

3 miles (5 km)   Easy; navigation is tricky

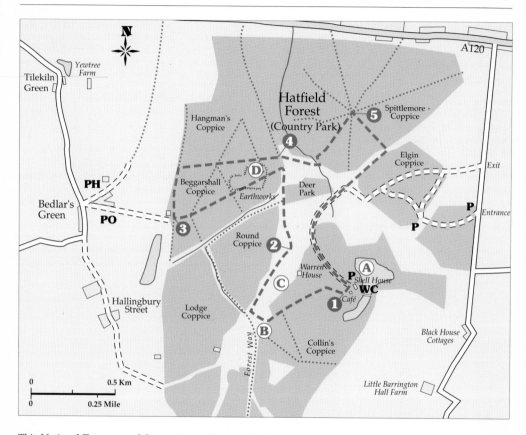

This National Trust owned forest attracts thousands of visitors, but only a short distance from the road the strange 'unmodernised' landscape evokes the medieval era when it was moulded. Not all paths are delineated, so a compass would be useful. To reach the start of the route, leave the M25 at junction 27 and drive north on the M11. Come off the motorway at junction 8 (Bishop's Stortford) and take the A120 east (under the M11) for 2 miles (3.2 km), then turn right along a lane signposted to Hatfield Forest. A short way down there is a car entrance on the right (charge to non-National Trust members). Drive along the road inside the boundary (open to cars Easter–end Oct only—in winter you must park at the edge of the forest) and continue until reaching the final car park near a lake and the Shell House Information Centre. PUBLIC TRANSPORT: Trains from London Liverpool Street to Bishop's Stortford connect with Eastern National bus 33 (Mon-Sat) and bus 133 (Mon-Sat and infrequent service Sun), which go via Stansted airport north of the forest road to Takeley village. (Walk west from Takeley for one mile (1.6 km), then turn left off the A120 and proceed for 0.6 miles (1 km) to the entrance gate.) Biss Bros bus 317 from Bishop's Stortford serves the A120 above the forest Mon-Sat, but only runs three times daily each way.

Route description

1 With your back to the lake, walk straight across the middle of the car park and proceed along a broad path. At a T-junction (ahead is not so much a path as a large unforested area grazed by cattle and stretching as far as the eye can see to the left and right), turn right but keep to the left-hand side of the clearing. Pass the small white gate to Warren House on your right.

2 Shortly after the access road becomes visible below you ahead, bear left towards the trees. Go through the gateway and continue past the wooden post, ignoring the left-hand path. At the next post (numbered 11), turn left and proceed past post 12 beside a small earthworks. Go straight over the next crossroads and over another clearer crossroads, continuing until you arrive at a T-junction at the back of a brick building.

3 Turn right along the edge of the forest with a field on your left and continue until reaching a stile ahead. Do not go over the stile, but turn right. On reaching a broad path across your route, maintain your direction, bearing slightly left to the path leading ahead. Go straight over the next junction and continue until you emerge into a clearing.

4 Bear slightly to the right down the gentle slope, passing an isolated group of ash trees on your left. A wooden post should soon come into view ahead. Walk to the post, then bear left down to a bridge over a stream. On the far side, turn sharp left and proceed a short distance to a stile. Do not go over the stile ahead but turn to the right and go over the stile here. Proceed ahead, with sparse ash and oak trees on your left and thicker forest on your right.

5 At the junction marked by three conifers, take the second path on the right. Go over the stile in the fence ahead, then turn right over another stile and proceed ahead. The path opens out into an area of open terrain and the access road comes into view ahead. Maintain your direction down to the road, then go right (effectively straight ahead) along the road. Keep going until you get back to the car park where you started.

Points of interest

A The largest lake in the forest park was created by damming a brook and was modelled by Capability Brown in 1757-9. He may also have designed the lakeside Shell House, which was built for the forest's private owner as a 'picnic house' at about the same time. It is literally covered in shells, corals and sand from the West Indies. Day permits are available for fishing in the lake and there is a refreshments hut and toilet. This lakeside area is often crowded with picnickers, some of whom stray no further into the forest!

B Despite attempts to create a landscaped park in the 18th century (as is apparent at **A**), Hatfield Forest retains all the elements of a medieval forest. It is mentioned in the Domesday Book of 1086 and became a Royal Forest for a short period in the 12th century. It then passed into private hands and rights over the forest were fiercely disputed for many years between landowners living on either side of it, thereby preventing exploitation of the land. Fallow deer were introduced and protected by by-laws, whilst local people continued to enjoy commoners' rights. In common with Epping Forest (see Walk 31), Hatfield was managed through grazing, coppicing and pollarding, and—uniquely—it still is. Hatfield Forest was owned by the Houblon family (Huguenot descendants of the first Governor of the Bank of England) for two centuries before it was left to the National Trust in 1924. Much of the so-called 'forest' is not densely planted but is more like scrub or downland.

C The old drovers' London Road runs across the forest from the north-east to the south-west. It is as broad as a field and is probably little changed from the medieval road.

D These earthworks show evidence of an Iron Age farm. There are a number of ancient mounds in the forest, one of which was made into an artificial rabbit warren in the 17th century, when it was popular to breed rabbits for their meat and fur.

Walk 33
ONGAR AND GREENSTED

3.5 miles (5.5 km)   Easy

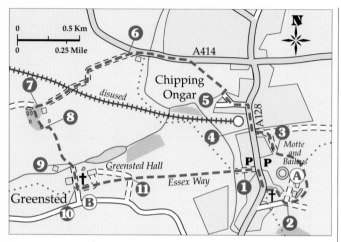

A fairly short walk through gently undulating countryside within easy reach of north and east London. To reach the start of the route, get onto the M11 in north-east London, then leave the motorway at the Chigwell exit inside the M25 and take the A113 north-east 10 miles (16 km) to Chipping Ongar. Drive into the town centre and park in one of the 'pay and display' car parks either side of the main road by Budworth Hall and The Cock Tavern. PUBLIC TRANSPORT: Take the Underground to Epping station (central line), and from there bus 201 or 501 to Chipping Ongar (infrequent service on Sun).

Route description

1 From the car park, walk towards the town centre then turn left by Ye Olde Corner Shoppe, following the sign to St Martin's Church. Follow the path to the left of the church, then fork right beside the 'White House'.

2 At the road, turn left and take the footpath between two driveways, which leads around the left-hand edge of the field. Past the farm entrance, turn left at the sign for 'Ongar Castle'. Ignore the left turn signposted to Ongar Town and continue to the end of the field.

3 Turn left and cross the stile in the corner onto a path which becomes a gravel track and then a lane. Bear left down to the main road.

4 Turn right and walk along the pavement for a short distance. Before the main road bends to the right, turn left into Bowes Drive then first right into Mark's Avenue. Follow the road to its end.

5 Take the footpath ahead, turning right to follow the right-hand edge of the field. Ignore turn-offs into adjoining playing field and aim for the white house on the roadside ahead. Eventually, a path on the left leads up to a metal gate onto the road. Turn left along the busy main road. When the pavement ends, cross the road (minding the traffic) and continue along the pavement on the other side until you reach Ruggles Restaurant on the left.

6 Walk up the gravel bridleway beside the restaurant, which gradually winds up the hill between hedges. Continue across the bridge over a disused railway and on to a house, where the track narrows and enters a copse.

7 Turn left soon into the trees (the turn-off may be hard to see through the undergrowth). Walk up to the stile ahead and climb over it into a field.

8 Bear left, past a willow tree and along the edge of the field, then down a grassy avenue between two cultivated fields.

9 At the corner of the second field, follow the path to the left. Take the right fork up a track leading to a farm. Go through the farmyard towards the metal gate and the white tower of the church.

10 Go through the gate and turn left into the entrance to Greensted Hall. As the drive bends to the left, go through the white gate into a field ahead. Proceed through the field, continue along the left-hand edge of the next field, then go through the gate in the fence ahead.

11 Cross over the tarmac drive and proceed to the stile ahead. Climb over it and and walk straight on through the field. At the bottom of the valley, cross the bridge over the stream and walk up to the main road, where the walk began.

Points of interest

A A moated 'mound' covered in trees to the left of the path is all that remains of a 12th-century castle.

B St Andrew's Church in Greensted is the oldest wooden church in England and the only remaining Anglo-Saxon church. The walls were constructed from split tree trunks in the 10th century, although the brick chancel and white timber tower were added later.

Walk 34
THORNDON COUNTRY PARK

3 miles (5 km) Easy
(but path surface is uneven in the woods)

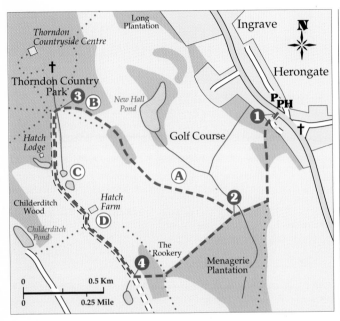

A short route through mixed woodland beside scrub and fallow fields affording distant views across the Essex countryside. To reach the start of the route, leave the M25 at junction 28 and take the A1023 into Brentwood, then get onto the A128 and drive south out of town, through Ingrave and into Herongate. At The Green Man pub on the left, turn left to park in the cul-de-sac in front of the pub. PUBLIC TRANSPORT: Take a train from London Liverpool Street to Brentwood, then Thamesway bus 151 from Brentwood High Street to Herongate (Mon-Sat only).

Route description

1 Cross the road from The Green Man pub and take the roughly surfaced track ahead (Park Lane). As the track bears left, go ahead across the grass and over a stile into the woods. Proceed along the path ahead, through woodland and then scrub. At a junction with another path, turn right (signposted to Childerditch Street) into more woods. Follow the path to a steep dip which bridges over a stream, and continue up the slope beyond it.

2 Turn right at the yellow arrow, over a small plank bridge and along a clear path which leads between uncultivated fields on the left and a golf course on your right. Continue ahead until the path eventually bends around to the right by a group of silver birches. Follow the path through a strip of woodland, then bear left out of the woods at a yellow arrow. Enter the edge of more woods at another yellow arrow.

3 At a signposted junction, bear left and—as the path straightens to continue ahead—turn left at the sign for Hatch Farm, along a gravel track with a wooden fence on your left. Pass Hatch Lodge (with an attractive pond in the grounds) on your right and two natural ponds on your left. Continue past Hatch Farm on your left, ignoring a turn-off on the right.

4 Take the next left turn (signposted) along a grassy path which leads into woods. At the next signpost, bear left to go straight on (follow the yellow arrow again), then bear right into the trees at the next yellow arrow. Proceed along the edge of the coniferous woodland, ignoring other paths on your right, until you eventually meet up with **2**. Continue straight on down the steep slope to retrace your steps back to the start.

Points of interest

A The golf course is on former private parkland which had been landscaped by Capability Brown.

B This area across the centre of the country park used to be farmed, but is now owned by The Woodland Trust, a nationwide organisation which has undertaken a tree planting project to extend the scrub, park and woodland that is preserved in the surrounding managed land.

C These attractive ponds are a recurring feature of Thorndon Country Park—look out for moorhens and ducks.

D Notice the interesting classical architecture of the brick buildings at Hatch Farm.

Walk 35
BENFLEET AND LEIGH

7 miles (11 km)
Easy outward route; moderate return

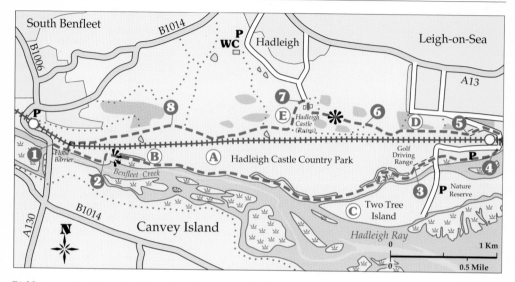

Richly rewarding for naturalists and with a man-made focus in Hadleigh Castle, this route may be followed in full or cut in half—the outward route is in itself a satisfying and very easy walk on level ground and the return may be made by train. To reach the start of the route, leave the M25 at junction 29 and drive east on the A127 for 11 miles (17.7 km). Then go south on the A130 for a short way before turning left onto the A13 and first right into South Benfleet. Continue down to Benfleet Creek and park in the 'pay and display' car park by the station. PUBLIC TRANSPORT: Trains run regularly from London Fenchurch Street direct to Benfleet (and Leigh).

Route description

1 Start the walk off the main road south of the station (turn left at the bend just before the bridge to Canvey Island). An initally tar-macked track leads past the flood barrier and on beside the water's edge, where leisure craft are moored.

2 Follow the track when it bends left through a car park. Climb over the stile beside the gate marked 'Hadleigh Castle Country Park', then continue parallel to the creek, above marshes and a dyke on the left. Continue for 2.3 miles (3.8 km) to the edge of Leigh.

3 Approaching the road bridge to Two Tree Island, the track becomes a tarmacked drive which leads past a driving range on your left. Climb over the stile at the end of the drive, cross the road and continue straight ahead on the path beside a boatyard and moorings. Go straight over the next crossroads, passing a green and car park, and continue along the raised path parallel to the road.

4 Cross the road where it bends inland and walk up the pavement, past the station. Turn left (through the bus depot) and walk along the edge of the main road until reaching a footpath sign on the left. Go down the gravel track and cross the stile into a field at the end.

5 Follow the path to the top of the field, then continue above the field, parallel to the railway line (ignore the right fork leading uphill). Continue ahead, ignoring left and right turns. (The path bears slightly towards the railway, then leads back towards the castle ruins.)

6 At the end of the field, go over the stile and up the hill. Proceed to the castle ruins, climb the stile in front of them and continue through the middle of the site, exit-ing at the right-hand corner to continue down a grassy path and through a metal gate. Turn left and climb over the stile on the left by the footpath sign.

7 Descend the hill on the gravel path and at the bottom turn right at the first gate (do not pass through the gate). Follow the footpath sign pointing over a stile and through the middle of a cultivated field. When the path ends, climb over the stile on the right and continue in the same direction, ignoring the uphill path on the right.

8 Follow the path when it bears left and leads over a stile by a 'Hadleigh Castle Country Park' sign. Then continue ahead, ignoring all turn-offs (follow the South Benfleet sign at the three-way post) until eventually reaching a kissing gate with a large pond beyond on the left. Pass through the gate and continue, going through another gate and on beside the railway track until the path ends. Cross the railway track via metal stiles, then turn right and retrace your steps to the start.

Points of interest

A Most of the walk takes place inside Hadleigh Castle Country Park, which was once entirely wooded and used as a royal hunting ground. Most of the woodland was cleared in the 14th and 15th centuries. It has since been used as grazing land and has been open to the public since 1987. The park contains some valuable wildlife habitats, described below.

B Benfleet salt marshes are carefully managed to support a wealth of unusual plants and insects which may be observed in the boggy pasture just off the path. The range of butterflies (including tortoiseshells, meadow browns and the rare marbled white), dragonflies (look out for the emperor—the largest species in Britain) and damselflies (emerald damselflies, once thought to be extinct in Essex, flourish here) is striking. The return route along the inland edge of the marsh provides further opportunities to see wildlife along a series of ditches and small ponds. Look out also for herons.

C Two Tree Island is an essential diversion for dedicated bird-watchers. The eastern part of the island is a nature reserve, where mud flats provide a valuable feeding and roosting ground for Brent geese and waders including curlews and redshanks.

D The pasture and scrub of the hills support nesting birds (including kestrels), mammals and butterflies.

E The remains of Hadleigh Castle now comprise the ruins of mid 14th-century towers presiding over remnants of stables and accommodation blocks. The castle was obsolete by the 16th century and was subsequently quarried for building stone. Fine views of the south-east tower may be seen early in the walk as well as on the approach, and from the hilltop site one can look over the surrounding countryside.

BARTHOLOMEW WALK GUIDES

Bartholomew publishes an extensive range of Walk Guides covering some of the best walking country in Britain, and further afield in France.

Titles in the series include:

Walk the Cornish Coastal Path
Walk the Cotswolds
Walk the Dales
Walk Dorset & Thomas Hardy's Wessex
Walk Kent
Walk the Lakes
Walk Loch Lomond & the Trossachs
Walk Loch Ness & the Spey Valley
Walk the New Forest
Walk the North York Moors
Walk Northumbria
Walk Oban, Mull & Lochaber
Walk the Peak District
Walk Perthshire
Walk Skye & Wester Ross
Walk Snowdonia & North Wales
Walk South Devon Coastal Path & Dartmoor

Walking in Brittany
Walking in the Dordogne
Walking in the Loire Valley
Walking in Provence

All titles are available from good bookshops, or telephone HarperCollins Distribution Services on 0141-772 3200.